British Red Cross

The —— RED CROSS STORY ——

Emily Wood

featuring a message from
Her Majesty The Queen
Patron and President of the British Red Cross

DORLING KINDERSLEY

A DORLING KINDERSLEY BOOK

Deputy Art Director
Tina Vaughan

Managing Editor
Jemima Dunne

Managing Art Editor
Philip Gilderdale

Designers
Steve Wooster
Karen Ward

Editors
Jackie Dobbyne
Janice Lacock

DTP Designer
Karen Ruane

Contributions from:
Lady Limerick (Sylvia), Chairman of Council
Mike Whitlam, Director General
John Gray, Director of Public Affairs
Alison Kearns, Archivist
Mark O'Brien, Executive Assistant to John Gray

First published in Great Britain in 1995
by Dorling Kindersley Limited,
9 Henrietta Street, London WC2E 8PS

A CIP catalogue record for this book is available
from the British Library.

ISBN 0 7513 0173 6 (Paperback)
ISBN 0 7513 0242 2 (Hardback)

Reproduced by Chroma Graphics (Overseas) Pte., Ltd in Singapore
Printed by New Interlitho in Italy

CONTENTS

A message from
Her Majesty The Queen *4*

FOUNDATION AND STRUCTURE 5

*A chronicle of the origins and foundation of the International Red Cross
and Red Crescent Movement, and of the British Red Cross*

EMERGENCY RELIEF WORK 23

*A review of the range of emergency relief work undertaken by
the British Red Cross at home and overseas
during the last 125 years*

WORK IN THE COMMUNITY 61

*An overview of the role that the British Red Cross plays in improving
health, preventing disease and mitigating suffering in the community*

FINANCE AND PATRONAGE 73

*How the British Red Cross raises funds and allocates them, as well
as an appreciation of the contribution made by the Royal Family
and other famous personalities*

FUTURE OF THE SOCIETY 89

The changing role of the British Red Cross and its aims for the future

INDEX *94*

ACKNOWLEDGMENTS *96*

A MESSAGE FROM
HER MAJESTY THE QUEEN

The Red Cross, born from the horrors of war, is a
society based on charity, compassion and the sanctity
of life. That the British Red Cross should have
flourished now for one hundred and twenty five years,
and have become one of the world's most powerful
agents for the relief and prevention of suffering, not
only in war but in peacetime too, is surely a cause
for celebration and national pride. The story of
the origins and development of the British Red Cross
deserves a wide hearing and it is one with which
I am pleased to be associated.

As we remember the self-sacrifice of celebrated
volunteers and marvel at the energies that so many have
devoted to the welfare of others, I hope that young
people everywhere are inspired to continue to shape
the Society in the future.

ELIZABETH R

Her Majesty The Queen
Patron and President of the British Red Cross

1

FOUNDATION AND STRUCTURE

This first chapter recalls the foundation of the Red Cross and Red Crescent Movement and the origins of the British Red Cross in particular. It describes the foundation of the International Committee of the Red Cross and the function of the International Federation of Red Cross and Red Crescent Societies. The individuals who have played a major role in shaping the British Red Cross are identified, as are some of the medal-winners and award-holders who personify the aims of the Society. Finally, the chapter examines the structure of the Society today.

THE ORIGINS OF THE RED CROSS MOVEMENT

THE EMBLEM OF the red cross or red crescent on a white background is recognized the world over as a symbol of protection, relief and comfort. It is the badge of an international, voluntary, humanitarian organization: the International Red Cross and Red Crescent Movement.

1828-1910 HENRY DUNANT

Henry Dunant (right), whose reaction to the appalling casualties of the Battle of Solferino led to the foundation of the Red Cross Movement.

1859 THE BATTLE OF SOLFERINO

A scene from the battle on 24 June 1859, during which many of the 40,000 casualties died for lack of care.

The origins of the Red Cross Movement stem from the Battle of Solferino, fought in Italy between Austria and the alliance of France and Sardinia in 1859. Henry Dunant, a young Swiss businessman, was appalled by the suffering of the wounded and dying on both sides. He galvanized local people into tending the wounded, regardless of their nationality. Two years later, he wrote an account of his experience, *A Memory of Solferino*, which was published in 1862. In his book, Dunant proposed an idea that eventually led to the formation of the Red Cross Movement. "Would it not be possible," he asked, "to form relief societies… for training volunteers to care for the wounded in wartime… based on some international principle…"

As a direct response to this plea, a committee headed by Gustave Moynier convened a conference of states, in Geneva in 1863, to consider the role of relief societies and their acceptance by military authorities. The conference was attended by delegations from 16 countries, including Great Britain. It passed ten resolutions for the organization and operation of relief societies and recommended the neutrality of army medical services and those under their care.

THE GENEVA CONVENTION

On 22 August 1864, the delegates from 12 states signed the Convention of Geneva "for the amelioration of the condition of the wounded in armies in the field". By 1867, all 16 states had ratified or acceded to the Convention, except for the United States, who did so in 1882. In 1875, the Geneva Committee became the International Committee. Dunant's idea of voluntary relief societies also struck a chord in many countries. The first society was formed in 1863 in Würtemburg, and soon there were over 30 in Europe and America.

For Dunant, the triumph was short-lived. His business ventures failed and, in 1867, he was declared bankrupt. Shortly after, he retired into obscurity. He was rediscovered in destitution as an old man and was awarded the Nobel Peace Prize in 1901. Dunant was delighted to receive the honour and recognition the award brought although he never used the prize money of 10,400 French francs. He died nine years later in October 1910.

1864 SIGNING THE GENEVA CONVENTION

12 delegates from Baden, Belgium, Denmark, France, Hesse, Italy, The Netherlands, Portugal, Prussia, Spain, Switzerland and Würtemburg signed the Geneva Convention. The representatives from Great Britain, Saxony, Sweden and the United States, although in full agreement, had not yet received authority to do so.

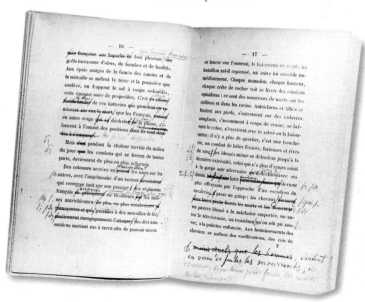

1863 UN SOUVENIR DE SOLFERINO

Corrections in Henry Dunant's hand to the third edition of A Memory of Solferino, *published in 1863.*

THE ESTABLISHMENT OF THE MOVEMENT

THE INTERNATIONAL COMMITTEE of the Red Cross, whose governing assembly is composed of a maximum of 25 Swiss citizens, is a private, neutral, independent institution that operates in armed conflicts and situations of internal violence to protect and assist the victims. Its role is defined in the four Geneva Conventions of 1949 (see opposite) and the two Additional Protocols of 1977.

THE FUNDAMENTAL PRINCIPLES OF THE RED CROSS AND RED CRESCENT MOVEMENT

Humanity
•
Impartiality
•
Neutrality
•
Independence
•
Voluntary service
•
Unity
•
Universality

PROVIDING PROTECTION

The International Committee of the Red Cross provides protection for war victims throughout the world.

Following the end of World War I, there was widespread chaos throughout much of Europe. It was as a response to the need to create a body capable of co-ordinating large-scale relief in peacetime that Henry Davison, President of the War Committee of the American Red Cross, proposed "to federate the Red Cross Societies of the different countries into an organization comparable to the League of Nations, in view of a worldwide

crusade to improve health, prevent sickness and alleviate suffering".
His plans were supported by the Red Cross Societies of Great
Britain, France, Italy, Japan and the United States who together
prepared a programme for worldwide preservation and improvement
of public health. In May 1919, the League of Red Cross Societies
(since 1991 called the International Federation of Red Cross and
Red Crescent Societies) was established. The Federation's role today
is to co-ordinate international relief for victims of natural disasters
and for refugees and displaced people outside conflict zones. It also
assists individual national societies with their development.

GENEVA CONVENTIONS

Since 1949 there have been four Geneva Conventions for the
Protection of War Victims which have been adopted by virtually
every country in the world. The aim of the original Convention
of 1864 was to improve the condition of the wounded of armies in
the field. In 1907, a Convention, agreed at The Hague, adapted
previous provisions to cover the wounded of maritime warfare.
A further Convention, adopted in 1929, detailed acceptable
treatment of prisoners of war, while a Convention of 1949 provided
for the protection of civilians in time of war. Two new treaties,
called Protocols, were drawn up in 1977. These add to and
update the 1949 Geneva Conventions, taking into account
modern means of warfare and aiming to give greater
protection to civilians. It is the work of the International
Committee to develop the Geneva Conventions and the
entire Movement has a key role in their promotion
throughout the world.

RED CROSS AND RED CRESCENT EMBLEMS

The emblem of a red cross on a white background was
created for a specific purpose: to ensure the protection
of the wounded in war and those who care for them.
The use of the emblem is regulated by international
law and all states party to the Geneva Conventions
must control its use nationally. It may only be displayed
on vehicles, aircraft, ships, buildings and installations
assigned to transport and shelter the wounded, or worn
by the personnel who care for them. National Red Cross
societies are permitted to use the emblem to identify
their premises, vehicles, equipment and personnel.

Although the red cross emblem has no religious
significance whatsoever, a red crescent emblem was
adopted by the Turks during the Serbo-Turkish War
of 1876. This symbol has since been adopted by a
number of countries in the Islamic world and since
1929 has been accepted as having equal status with
the red cross emblem.

GIVING HUMANITARIAN AID

*The International Red Cross and Red
Crescent Movement provides
humanitarian aid to the most vulnerable
people worldwide.*

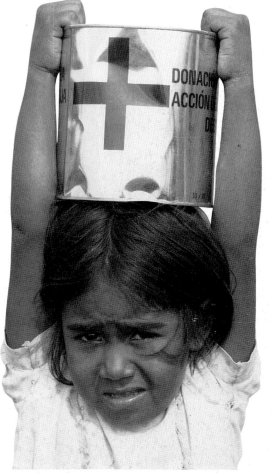

THE BEGINNINGS OF THE BRITISH RED CROSS

ON 15 JULY 1870, war was declared between France and
Germany. In Great Britain there was sympathy for both sides:
the French had been a staunch ally during the Crimean War
of 1854–56 and the Princess Royal was shortly to marry
Prince Friedrich of Prussia, later Kaiser Wilhem II.

*"No-one could form any
notion of the greatness
and extent of the benefits
of the English Society"*

MRS ELPHINSTONE, WIFE OF
SOCIETY'S CHIEF COMMISSIONER
OF THE WESTERN DISTRICT

A week after the outbreak of the Franco-Prussian War, Colonel
Loyd-Lindsay, who had witnessed the suffering of soldiers in
the Crimea and believed that much of that suffering could have
been avoided and countless lives saved had a national society for the
sick and wounded in war been in existence in Britain, wrote a letter
to *The Times* calling for such a society to be formed in Great Britain.
He wrote: "During every war the want of medical comforts has
been sorely felt… England is, fortunately, neutral, and for that
reason can show her sympathy with both nations, through the sick
and wounded, who have done nothing to deserve their hard fate…

We should form a Committee… and
place ourselves in communication with
the other Committees already formed all
over Europe, in order that what we do
may be done fairly and impartially
between the belligerents." At the same
time, Loyd-Lindsay wrote to eminent
people of the day to gain their support.
Florence Nightingale replied that he was
"quite on the right tack".

At a public meeting held in London
on 4 August, a resolution was passed that
"a National Society be formed in this
country for aiding sick and wounded
soldiers in time of war and that the said

1870 SCENE FROM THE
FRANCO-PRUSSIAN WAR

*The plight of the wounded in the
Franco-Prussian War prompted many
offers of help. Just one month after the
outbreak of the war, the Society had
40 surgeons working with the wounded.*

Society be formed upon the Rules laid down by the Geneva
Convention of 1864… That the Society adopt the Badge and Flag
which have been recognized by the International Convention of
Geneva." The society known today as the British Red Cross was born.

A committee of 22 was formed with Loyd-Lindsay as Chairman,
Queen Victoria as Patron and the Prince of Wales, later Edward VII,
as President. Queen Victoria's daughter, Princess Christian, became

Colonel Loyd-Lindsay leaving the German lines at Versailles to deliver money to the French authorities in Paris. He is followed by his manservant, Mr Whittle, who is carrying the money in his bag.

Chairman of the Ladies' Committee. Local committees were formed in almost every town and district of Great Britain and goods poured in from Australia, China and India. Thousands of bales of linen and clothes, surgical instruments, chloroform and morphia, as well as surgeons, nurses and agents, were sent to the areas of conflict.

1870 THE LADIES' COMMITTEE

The members of the Ladies' Committee included Florence Nightingale, The Honorable Mrs Loyd-Lindsay, Princess Christian of Schleswig-Holstein and Princess Mary of Teck.

THE FIRST APPEAL

By the end of March 1871, nearly £300,000 had been raised. The Committee decided to give £40,000 in cash directly to both sides. Loyd-Lindsay was given the task of carrying this gift in equal proportions to the Germans at Versailles and to the French in Paris. He later wrote: "The fact that I was conducted through the lines of advanced posts by a Prussian officer on my way to bring help to the French sick and wounded could only have occurred under the protection of, and in the spirit of, the Geneva Convention… the white flag with a red cross was honoured by soldiers and patients alike."

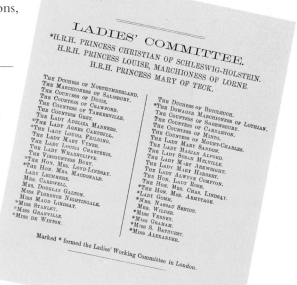

LADIES' COMMITTEE.

*H.R.H. PRINCESS CHRISTIAN OF SCHLESWIG-HOLSTEIN.
H.R.H. PRINCESS LOUISE, MARCHIONESS OF LORNE.
H.R.H. PRINCESS MARY OF TECK.

THE DUCHESS OF NORTHUMBERLAND.
THE MARCHIONESS OF SALISBURY.
THE COUNTESS OF DUCIE.
THE COUNTESS OF CRAWFORD.
THE COUNTESS OF TANKERVILLE.
THE COUNTESS GREY.
THE LADY ADELIZA MANNERS.
*THE LADY AGNES CAMPBELL.
THE LADY MARY VYNER.
THE LADY LOUISA FEILDING.
THE LADY LOUISA CHARTERIS.
THE VISCOUNTESS BURY.
*THE HON. MRS. LOYD-LINDSAY.
*THE HON. MRS. MACDONALD.
LADY LECHMERE.
MRS. CARDWELL.
MRS. DOUGLAS GALTON.
MISS FLORENCE NIGHTINGALE.
MISS MAUD LINDSAY.
*MISS STANLEY.
*MISS GRANVILLE.
*MISS DE WINTON.

THE DUCHESS OF BUCCLEUCH.
*THE DOWAGER MARCHIONESS OF LOTHIAN.
THE COUNTESS OF SHREWSBURY.
THE COUNTESS OF CARNARVON.
THE COUNTESS OF MINTO.
THE LADY MARY SANDON.
THE LADY MARIAN ALFORD.
THE LADY SUSAN MELVILLE.
THE LADY MARY ARKWRIGHT.
THE LADY MARY HERBERT.
THE LADY ALWYNE COMPTON.
THE HON. LADY ROSE.
THE HON. MRS. CHAS. LINDSAY.
*THE HON. MRS. ARMITAGE.
*LADY GOMM.
*MRS. NASSAU SENIOR.
MRS. WILDER.
*MISS VERNEY.
*MISS GRAHAM.
*MISS S. BATHURST.
MISS ALEXANDER.

*Marked * formed the Ladies' Working Committee in London.*

KEY PERSONALITIES

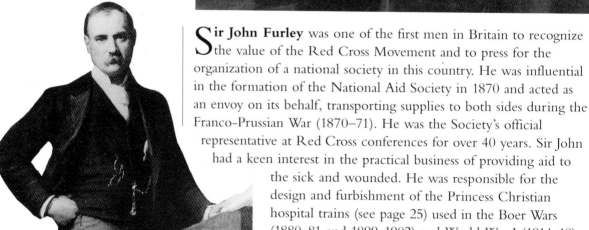

THE REAL STRENGTH of the British Red Cross Society lies in the people who realize its vital role and embrace its cause. Some individuals have had a profound effect on the development of the British Red Cross, leading it through periods of turmoil and peace, either by lending their influence to enhance its position, or by quietly getting on with the job.

1836-1919 JOHN FURLEY

Sir John Furley, CH, CB, a member of the Order of St John, was influential in the foundation of the National Aid Society, the forerunner of the British Red Cross.

Sir John Furley was one of the first men in Britain to recognize the value of the Red Cross Movement and to press for the organization of a national society in this country. He was influential in the formation of the National Aid Society in 1870 and acted as an envoy on its behalf, transporting supplies to both sides during the Franco-Prussian War (1870–71). He was the Society's official representative at Red Cross conferences for over 40 years. Sir John had a keen interest in the practical business of providing aid to the sick and wounded. He was responsible for the design and furbishment of the Princess Christian hospital trains (see page 25) used in the Boer Wars (1880–81 and 1899–1902) and World War I (1914–18); and the 500-bed extension to the hospital at Netley in Hampshire was constructed according to his recommendations. Throughout his time with the Red Cross, Sir John maintained his interest in the Order of St John and was one of the founders of the St John Ambulance Association. At his burial, his coffin was draped with the flags of both organizations.

1853-1923 FREDERICK TREVES

Sir Frederick Treves, Bart, GCVO, CB, surgeon to the Elephant Man, was closely involved in the reorganization of the British Red Cross.

Sir Frederick Treves is perhaps most widely known as the surgeon who treated John Merrick, the Elephant Man. However, his wartime experiences in the army medical services during the second Boer War convinced him of the need for a permanent Red Cross Society in Britain. His connections at court – he was surgeon to

Queen Victoria, King Edward VII and King George V – meant that he was an influential figure during the reorganization of the Red Cross in Britain in 1905. He had seen the work of the Red Cross Societies in Japan and Russia and reported on their work to Queen Alexandra and King Edward VII. Sir Frederick was elected as the first Executive Committee Chairman of the newly constituted British Red Cross Society in 1905. As such he was closely involved in the formation of the Voluntary Aid Detachment scheme (see pages 28–29) and widely promoted it through speeches and articles. Sir Frederick resigned the chairmanship in 1912. However, his interest in the choice and efficiency of the Society's personnel led him to become involved in the selection of staff sent abroad by the Society in both the Balkan War (1912–13) and World War I.

Sir Arthur Stanley served in high offices of the British Red Cross for over 40 years. He guided its actions through both world wars and its development during the intervening years of peace. As Chairman of the Executive Committee from 1914 to 1943 and Chairman of both the Joint War Committee and the Joint War Organization, his leadership was vital during times when the demands on the British Red Cross had never been greater. However, his keenest interest lay in the effect that the Red Cross could have on the relief of sickness and suffering in times of peace. He was a leading figure in the creation of the League of Red Cross and Red Crescent Societies (later the International Federation of Red Cross and Red Crescent Societies) with its emphasis on the relief of suffering in the aftermath of disaster or epidemics. He was involved in the establishment of the Red Cross Clinic for Rheumatic Diseases (later renamed the Arthur Stanley Institute for Rheumatic Diseases) in London and took a close interest in the foundation and administration of the Star & Garter Home for disabled sailors, soldiers and airmen in Richmond, Surrey. Sir Arthur was Chairman of the Royal College of Nursing and Treasurer of St Thomas's Hospital in London.

The British Red Cross also depends on the many hundreds of paid and volunteer workers who toil tirelessly on behalf of the Society at home and abroad. Many of these people are unsung heroes: men and women who have given their lives for others. One such was John McIntosh, a young man of 19 from Hamilton in Scotland who offered his services to the National Aid Society on 10 October 1870. He was sent to Germany as a dresser of wounds during the Franco-Prussian War of 1870–71. He is remembered today as the first member of the British Red Cross to lose his life while working for the Society.

1869 - 1947 ARTHUR STANLEY

Hon. Sir Arthur Stanley GCVO, GBE, CB, DL, JP, LLD, FRCP (hon), played a major role in the development of the British Red Cross for over 40 years.

1851-70 JOHN McINTOSH

John McIntosh, who died on 23 November 1870, in Saarbrucken, Germany, was the first British Red Cross member to die on active duty.

Angela, Countess of Limerick, was once described as "the very symbol of the Red Cross". Her service with the Movement spanned more than 60 years and, thanks to her exceptional human qualities, untiring activity and wisdom, she exerted a prominent influence. Angela Limerick joined the British Red Cross in 1915. Being too young for overseas service, she falsified her age to care for the wounded near the battlefront in France. In the following years, she became one of the most well-known and best-loved Red Cross leaders of all time. She led the British delegation at all of the international Red Cross conferences (1948–65) and was also Chairman of the Standing Commission (1965–73). Over 20 national societies honoured her and, in 1975, she received the highest International Red Cross distinction, the Henry Dunant medal. In 1976, after service as Vice Chairman of the Executive Committee and Chairman of Council, she was then appointed a Vice President, the first person outside the Royal Family to be approved by the Queen for such an appointment.

1898-1981 ANGELA LIMERICK

Angela Limerick, GBE, CH, DL, LLD (hon), seen here in 1954, devoted much of her life to both the British Red Cross and the International Movement.

1910- MURIEL MONKHOUSE

Although she officially retired in 1979, Muriel Monkhouse continues to give invaluable advice and assistance to the International Welfare Department.

1935- SYLVIA LIMERICK

Sylvia Limerick, CBE, D Litt (hon), FRCP (hon), is Chairman of Council.

Since 1985, the Chairman of Council of the British Red Cross has been Sylvia, Countess of Limerick. Encouraged by her mother-in-law, she joined the International Division in 1962 where she worked in the Tracing and Message Service. In 1993, she was also elected a Vice President of the International Federation of Red Cross and Red Crescent Societies.

Muriel Monkhouse's vital work, as Head of the French Civilian Tracing Section in the Foreign Relations Department of the Joint War Organization of the British Red Cross and Order of St John, was to relay messages between families separated by World War II. The essential guidelines she established for tracing and the delivery of Red Cross messages are still in use (see pages 68–69). In 1977 Muriel was awarded the OBE for her services and in 1979 she received the British Red Cross Society's Badge of Honour for Distinguished Service and life membership of the Society.

THE PRINCIPAL OBJECTIVES

THE RED CROSS SOCIETY in Britain was originally entitled the National Society for Aid to the Sick and Wounded in War. In 1898 a Central Red Cross Committee was formed under the guidance of the War Office. This Committee, whose members were drawn from various voluntary societies operating in the country, was an attempt by the War Office to ensure both closer co-operation with the Army Medical Service and to prevent any overlapping in duties. In 1905, the Central Red Cross Committee and the National Aid Society joined together to form the British Red Cross Society under the presidency of Queen Alexandra.

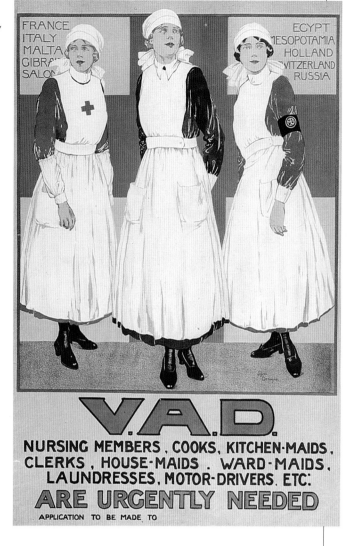

In its Royal Charter of Incorporation, granted in 1908, the Society's primary objective was defined as "to furnish aid to the sick and wounded in war". A year later, following the passing of the Territorial and Reserve Forces Act, the Society began establishing Voluntary Aid Detachments (VADs) in each county. It was these VADs who were to prove so vital during World Wars I and II (see pages 28–29).

When World War I ended in 1918 and demobilization was complete, the Society entered a new era in its history. In 1919, as a founder member of the League of Red Cross Societies, the British Red Cross petitioned for and obtained a Supplemental Charter. This widened the objectives of the Society to include the improvement of health, the prevention of disease and the mitigation of suffering throughout the world and thus enabled it to embark on a programme of humanitarian activities in peacetime. In 1990, the Society's Council approved a mission statement: "The British Red Cross gives skilled and impartial care to people in need and in crisis, in their own homes and in the community, at home and abroad, in peace and in war."

WORLD WAR I VAD
RECRUITMENT POSTER

This recruitment poster, drawn by a VAD, Joyce Dennys, was issued during World War I. It is believed to be the only one as the response was so great another was not necessary.

Medal-winners and Award-holders

WHETHER FOR EXCEPTIONAL SERVICE or for outstanding acts, the presentation of medals and awards is a long-standing tradition for the British Red Cross. Working for the Society requires a dedication to helping others in crisis, a dedication that Red Cross members always possess.

In times of emergency, conflict or disaster, working for the Red Cross demands an extra commitment to caring for others in the face of danger or trauma. Since 1911, the British Red Cross Society has issued a wide range of awards to identify members, to acknowledge

FLORENCE NIGHTINGALE MEDAL

This medal is awarded to nurses or voluntary aides for exceptional courage and devotion to the wounded, sick or disabled or to civilian victims of conflict or disaster.

EARLY RED CROSS AWARDS

Above is a selection of awards given for British Red Cross work: the War Medal, the Balkan War Medal and the Voluntary Medical Services Medal.

"FOR EXCEPTIONAL COURAGE AND DEVOTION"

Claire Bertschinger received the ICRC Florence Nightingale Medal from the Countess Mountbatten of Burma, a Vice President of the Society, in 1991.

CARE IN CRISIS AWARD

The Care in Crisis Award, launched in 1992, is given annually to people, nominated by members of the public, who have shown exceptional care to someone in crisis in their community.

exceptional, distinguished or devoted service, or to denote qualifications. It has produced two wartime awards: the Balkan War Medal, awarded to 268 people who worked for or assisted the Society during the war of 1912–13, and the War Medal, awarded to over 41,000 members who gave unpaid service in this country during World War I. The Voluntary Medical Services Medal (VMS) was instituted in 1932 and is still awarded to members with 15 years' qualifying service.

Members of the British Red Cross are eligible for official decorations from Great Britain and other countries, as well as for those awarded by the Red Cross and Red Crescent Movement. Other awards, such as The Florence Nightingale Medal, which is now given every two years by the International Committee of the Red Cross and is the highest award granted by the Committee for nursing the sick and wounded, can be made to individuals who are not members of any Red Cross Society.

The most recent award instituted by the British Red Cross is the Muriel Monkhouse Award. Launched in 1994, this award recognizes the invaluable work of volunteers who deliver the international tracing and message services (see pages 68–69). As such, it is an example of the importance the Society places on rewarding those who quietly get on with their work of helping people in crisis.

A COOL HEAD IN A CRISIS

In 1993, five-year-old Steven Lack received his Care in Crisis Award for saving his two-year-old brother's life when he fell into a fishpond. Steven kept his brother's face clear of the water while screaming for help.

THE STRUCTURE OF THE SOCIETY TODAY

THE ABILITY OF THE SOCIETY to undertake its whole range of services both at home and abroad relies on the strength of its internal structure. Developed through history into the efficient organisation it is today, this structure incorporates the governing body of the Council, national headquarters, branches and committees at home and overseas, and the membership.

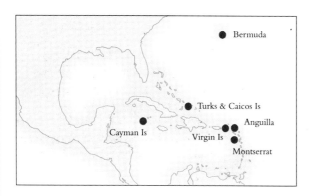

OVERSEAS BRANCHES IN THE CARIBBEAN

The British Red Cross has branches in Anguilla, Bermuda, the British Virgin Islands, the Cayman Islands, Montserrat and the Turks & Caicos Islands.

The Society's governing body is the *Council* which elects the Chairman, up to four Vice-Chairmen and up to 32 members from the Society. They represent the branches in England and Wales, Northern Ireland and Scotland, the medical, nursing and social services professions. Three members, aged between 18 and 25 at the time of election, are proposed by the National Youth Forum. The only non-Red Cross member of the Council is the Surgeon-General of the Medical Services of the Armed Forces, who is proposed by the Ministry of Defence. Since the British Red Cross is a registered charity, members of Council are Trustees of the Society, unpaid volunteers who are responsible for the proper management and administration of the Society. Observers from the Ministry of Defence and the Department of Health, and representatives from Hong Kong and the Isle of Man, also take part on occasion.

NATIONAL HEADQUARTERS

The headquarters of the Society is in London where the Director General, who is appointed by Council as the Chief Executive Officer, directs the headquarters' staff and ensures that the policies agreed by Council are implemented. The staff provide professional and technical guidance to the branches, ensuring that the services provided in local communities are of the highest possible standard, meet real needs and are efficiently managed. Staff at national headquarters are also responsible for the provision of international disaster relief, development programmes, and the international tracing service.

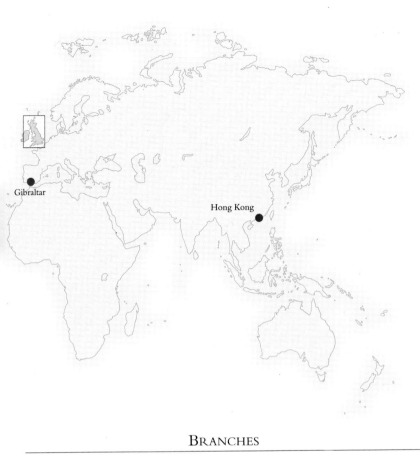

THE BRITISH RED CROSS WORLDWIDE

Overseas, the British Red Cross has a Central Council branch in Hong Kong, and overseas branches in the Falkland Islands, Gibraltar and the Caribbean (see far left). In this country, the Society has branches in England and Wales, Scotland and Northern Ireland. It is also represented in the Channel Islands and the Isle of Man (not shown).

BRANCHES

The Society has a branch in every county in England and Wales, a Central Council Branch, with local branches, in Scotland, Northern Ireland and the Isle of Man, and a branch and a committee in the Channel Islands. Each branch has a governing committee, director and specialist staff and is responsible for carrying out the work of the Society in its area, in accordance with the policies laid down by Council. The work is directed and guided using the volunteer membership who operate primarily from local centres. In 1995, the Society also has an Overseas Central Council Branch in Hong Kong and overseas branches or committees in eight other British territories.

MEMBERSHIP

The Society has a combined adult and youth membership approaching 100,000 volunteers. Members of the British Red Cross have agreed to abide by the principles of the Red Cross and Red Crescent Movement and the rules of the Society. As members, they have also agreed to give a minimum of 10 hours' service per year, with the vast majority giving much more. In 1994, it was estimated that British Red Cross members gave five million hours of their time to community work in the United Kingdom, equivalent to £24 million. Many members, once committed, continue to give service for many years and it is not unusual for someone to work with the Society for 50 years.

Overseas Branches

BRITISH RED CROSS MEMBERS brought the ideals of the Red Cross Movement with them as they settled overseas. The formation of national Red Cross/Red Crescent societies around the world owes much to the activities of these dedicated individuals.

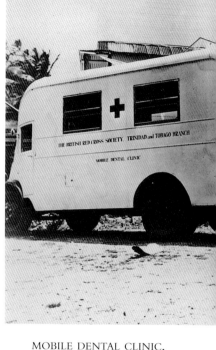

GIFT FROM THE PEOPLE OF THE GOLD COAST

This diorama was presented in 1950 to the Gold Coast Branch, one of the early overseas branches of the British Red Cross.

MOTHER & BABY GROUP, MALAWI

Health education, clinics and mother and baby groups, such as this one in 1966, became prominent features of overseas branch work.

Red Cross groups formed within the British Empire were necessarily affiliated to the British Red Cross. At the outbreak of World War I, British Red Cross branches were formed in Australia, Canada, India, New Zealand and South Africa. More branches were formed in Africa in the 1930s, and after World War II it was the aim of the Society to form a branch in every colony and protectorate.

MOBILE DENTAL CLINIC, TRINIDAD AND TOBAGO

The British Red Cross provided this mobile dental clinic in 1948 on Tobago.

WELFARE WORK

Overseas branches carried out similar peacetime work to county branches in Britain. However, the emphasis on welfare work was particularly strong as the Red Cross often supplemented meagre local provision. In areas where communications were poor or distances vast, a Red Cross water or air ambulance, mobile clinic or district health visitor formed an important part of the community's health provision.

Where natural disasters such as floods, hurricanes, typhoons and earthquakes regularly occur, overseas branches played a vital role in providing relief and co-operating in disaster preparedness schemes.

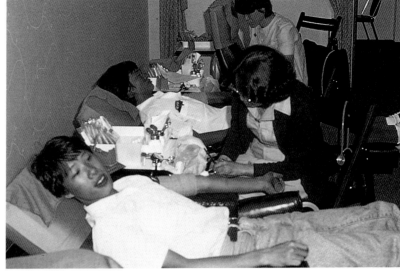

HONG KONG

Among many other services, the Hong Kong branch operates the Blood Transfusion Service.

AFRICAN BLOOD DONOR,
NORTH RHODESIA

The Ndola divison of the Rhodesian branch spearheaded a drive for blood donors to supply the local hospital.

HYGIENE AND SANITATION

This poster was one of many health education posters produced by the overseas branches.

From 1947 the Society provided significant aid to its overseas branches although its aim was to involve citizens in running their own Red Cross branch. After a country became independent the evolution of its national society was overseen by the Development Programme at the League.

WASH YOUR HANDS ALWAYS

BRITISH RED CROSS SOCIETY JUNIOR · SERVE ONE ANOTHER

E.O.Hanson

BEFORE EATING

INTERNATIONAL FAMILY TREE

THIS "FAMILY TREE" celebrates the growth of the International Movement to 1914. The formation dates of all 163 currently recognized national societies are listed below.

Afghanistan	9 April 1934
Albania	4 October 1921
Algeria	11 January 1963
Andorra	Unknown
Angola	16 March 1978
Antigua & Barbuda	Unknown
Argentina	10 June 1880
Australia	13 August 1914
Austria	14 March 1880
Bahamas	16 November 1939
Bahrain	28 January 1970
Bangladesh	31 March 1973
Barbados	17 February 1960
Belgium	4 February 1864
Belize	12 April 1950
Benin	1 May 1963
Bolivia	27 May 1880
Botswana	1 March 1968
Brazil	5 December 1908
Bulgaria	25 October 1878
Burkina Faso	31 July 1961
Burundi	29 July 1963
Cambodia	18 February 1955
Cameroon	9 January 1963
Canada	19 May 1909
Cape Verde	3 November 1984
Central African Rep.	25 October 1966
Chad	1 June 1983
Chile	18 December 1903
China	29 May 1904
Colombia	23 July 1915
Congo	22 February 1964
Costa Rica	4 April 1885
Cote D'Ivoire	18 April 1963
Croatia	Unknown
Cuba	10 March 1909
Czech Republic	5 June 1993
Denmark	27 April 1876
Djibouti	1 August 1977
Dominica	7 April 1983
Dominican Republic	23 April 1927
Ecuador	22 April 1910
Egypt	24 October 1912
El Salvador	13 March 1885
Equatorial Guinea	Unknown
Estonia	Unknown
Ethiopia	8 July 1935
Fiji	27 September 1971
Finland	7 May 1877
France	25 May 1864
Gambia, The	1 October 1966
Germany, Fed. Rep. of	4 February 1950
Ghana	1 October 1957
Greece	10 June 1877
Grenada	21 August 1981
Guatemala	22 April 1923
Guinea	26 January 1984
Guinea-Bissau	2 December 1977
Guyana	30 December 1967
Haiti	29 May 1932
Honduras	24 September 1937
Hungary	27 March 1881
Iceland	10 December 1924
India	7 June 1920
Indonesia	17 September 1945
Iran, Islamic Rep. of	3 April 1923
Iraq	28 February 1932
Ireland	5 September 1939
Italy	15 June 1864
Jamaica	9 July 1964
Japan	1 May 1877
Jordan	12 January 1948
Kenya	21 December 1965
Korea, Dem. P. Rep.	18 October 1946
Korea, Rep.	27 October 1905
Kuwait	10 January 1966
Lao, P. Dem. Rep.	1 January 1955
Latvia	20 November 1918
Lebanon	9 July 1945
Lesotho	9 November 1967
Liberia	22 January 1919
Libyan Arab Jamahiriya	5 October 1957
Liechtenstein	30 April 1945
Lithuania	1919
Luxembourg	8 August 1914
Madagascar	19 May 1959
Malawi	13 January 1967
Malaysia	22 November 1957
Mali	24 August 1965
Malta	Unknown
Mauritania	4 March 1971
Mauritius	18 December 1973
Mexico	21 February 1910
Monaco	3 March 1948
Mongolia	16 June 1939
Morocco	24 December 1957
Mozambique	17 May 1988
Myanmar	1 April 1937
Namibia	Unknown
Nepal	4 September 1963
Netherlands, The	19 July 1867
New Zealand	22 December 1931
Nicaragua	10 January 1934
Niger	16 July 1963
Nigeria	29 September 1960
Norway	22 September 1865
Pakistan	20 December 1947
Panama	1 March 1917
Papua New Guinea	7 April 1977
Paraguay	12 November 1919
Peru	17 April 1879
Philippines	15 April 1947
Poland	27 April 1919
Portugal	11 February 1865
Qatar	27 August 1981
Romania	4 July 1876
Russian Federation	3 May 1867
Rwanda	29 December 1964
Saint Lucia	16 March 1949
Saint Vincent and The Grenadines	17 May 1984
Saint Kitts & Nevis	Unknown
Samoa	1952
San Marino	8 October 1949
Sao Tome & Principe	20 January 1976
Saudi Arabia	8 June 1963
Seychelles	1987
Senegal	29 January 1963
Sierra Leone	1 July 1962
Singapore	6 April 1973
Slovakia	Unknown
Slovenia	Unknown
Solomon Islands	6 July 1983
Somalia	27 April 1963
South Africa	1 January 1896
Spain	6 July 1864
Sri Lanka	1 August 1949
Sudan	30 October 1956
Surinam	20 June 1940
Swaziland	13 October 1970
Sweden	24 May 1865
Switzerland	17 July 1866
Syrian Arab Rep.	30 May 1942
Tanzania, Utd. Rep. of	7 December 1962
Thailand	26 April 1893
Togo	26 February 1959
Tonga	10 August 1972
Trinidad & Tobago	31 May 1963
Tunisia	7 October 1956
Turkey	11 June 1868
Uganda	30 July 1964
Ukraine	Unknown
United Arab Emirates	24 January 1983
United Kingdom	4 August 1870
United States of America	21 May 1881
Uruguay	5 March 1897
Vanuatu	30 July 1980
Venezuela	30 January 1895
Vietnam	23 November 1946
Yemen	16 July 1970
former Yugoslavia	25 January 1876
Zaire	1 July 1960
Zambia	22 April 1966
Zimbabwe	2 October 1981

2

EMERGENCY RELIEF WORK

This chapter gives a glimpse of the range of emergency relief work undertaken by the British Red Cross. It describes the aid given during many conflicts and natural disasters throughout the last 125 years; the vital contribution of the Voluntary Aid Detachments (VADs); the extension of the Society's charter to embrace peacetime activities, and the critical role of Red Cross parcels in World War II. The chapter also acknowledges the many unseen heroes, the Red Cross delegates who use their expertise to save others.

WORK IN THE EARLY DAYS 1876-1914

IN ITS EARLY DAYS, the Society's work was restricted to providing aid on the battlefield and to training the nurses who would work in conflicts overseas. "…Whenever we may be dragged into a serious war, your Society will be invaluable, and I very much doubt if our Government ever could render officially as much effective assistance to our sick and wounded as your Society could."

Field-Marshal Sir Carnet Wolseley 1877

1900 ITEMS FROM EARLY MEDICAL KIT

Early kits contained surgical instruments. Handmade charpie (shredded lint) was used as a dressing.

1884 THE QUEEN VICTORIA HOSPITAL LAUNCH

The use of the hospital launch Queen Victoria *in Egypt was the first time that the Society provided a complete unit to supplement the British Army Medical Services in time of war.*

1876 TURKEY AND SERBIA

In the summer of 1876 news reached England of the terrible suffering endured by the victims of the war between Turkey and Serbia. Public opinion was such that the British Red Cross offered help. Thirty-five surgeons, nurses and agents went out to the frontline, and stores of medicine, disinfectant and surgical supplies were sent to both sides. A hospital was set up in Belgrade which was, according to one doctor, "a model of what such a hospital should be". This was the first occasion on which the red crescent was used, by the Turks.

1877–1878 TURKEY AND RUSSIA

In April 1877, two months after the end of the Serbo-Turkish war, Turkey was in conflict with Russia. The Society chartered a small steamer to carry stores, equipment and surgeons to the Black Sea. *The Belle of Dunkerque* carried £7,000 worth of medical supplies that were distributed to both Turkish and Russian hospitals.

1879–1885 BOER REBELLION AND EGYPTIAN CAMPAIGN

During this period the British Red Cross provided medical supplies for use in the Zulu war, the Boer rebellion and

the Egyptian campaign. In 1882, 24 nurses selected by Florence Nightingale were sent to Egypt. The steamer *Queen Victoria* was bought by the Red Cross to tow a barge that transported patients and medical supplies up and down the Nile. It was so successful that two further steamers, *Alexandra* and *Princess*, were built.

1885–1898 SERBIA AND BULGARIA

The British Red Cross assisted in the Serbo-Bulgarian war of 1885–86 by supplying clothing, blankets and medical help. A hospital was set up in Belgrade which stored clothes and shoes to be supplied to field hospitals.

1897 TURKEY AND GREECE

In 1897 war broke out between Turkey and Greece. The British Red Cross decided that no personnel were required since the main problem was refugees. Food was distributed through various soup kitchens to alleviate starvation.

1899–1902 SOUTH AFRICA

When the second Boer War broke out in South Africa, the British Red Cross made a vital contribution through the provision of hospital trains. Since these trains supplied the wounded with clothing and toiletries, and removed the more seriously injured to Cape Town on the return journey, they became very popular. The hospital ship the *Princess of Wales* treated 728 casualties and covered about 40,000 miles carrying patients back to England as well as acting as a hospital outside Durban. The *Princess Christian*, the first purpose-built hospital train, which carried 7,548 badly injured soldiers, also made a great contribution to relieving the suffering of the wounded.

1912–1913 TURKEY AND THE BALKAN STATES

The war between Turkey and the Balkan states resulted in British Red Cross units being dispatched to Turkey, Greece, Montenegro, Serbia and Bulgaria. Medical supplies and hospital provisions to the value of £31,403 were sent to all the countries involved in this conflict.

1899 THE *PRINCESS CHRISTIAN* TRAIN

Standing in front of the Princess Christian *hospital train, used during the Boer War, is an orderly wearing tropical uniform.*

1899 PRINCESS CHRISTIAN DRINKING CUP

This drinking cup was once used by wounded soldiers on the Princess Christian *hospital train.*

WORLD WAR I 1914-18

THE OUTBREAK OF HOSTILITIES in 1914 was greeted with enthusiasm throughout Europe. Everyone believed that victory would be quick and decisive. Among the British, only Lord Kitchener foresaw a long struggle. He would be proved right: within two months, trench warfare, which would last four years, began on the Western Front.

"I can appreciate very fully what Red Cross aid means to the wounded…"

SIR JOHN GOODWIN, DIRECTOR-GENERAL, ARMY MEDICAL SERVICE

VAD MOTOR AMBULANCE DRIVERS

The first convoy of female VAD drivers went to France in April 1916 and proved so successful that a further 110 drivers were sent to Etaples, as seen below.

The British Red Cross responded to the outbreak of war by issuing an appeal for funds, offering to provide the War Office with a 500-bed hospital at Netley in Hampshire, and despatching a Commission to France which established hospitals in Paris and Rouen and began to meet the army's desperate need for the quick, efficient transport of wounded soldiers.

In 1914, the British Army still relied on horse-drawn ambulances. Such inadequate transport severely crippled the efforts of the Royal Army Medical Corps. Alfred Keogh, leader of the Commission, immediately recognized the life-saving potential of motorized transport. As a result, 20 motor cars were provided and in September 1914 a further eight ambulances and six cars were despatched to search for wounded men in villages unoccupied by the Germans.

Existing French rolling stock was transformed into two improvized hospital trains. In October, a third train was fitted out and more ambulances rushed to the battlefield. Shortly after, 16 VADs and two trained nurses established a rest station at Boulogne where they met trains of wounded on their way to the base hospital at Rouen.

THE JOINT WAR COMMITTEE

By the autumn of 1914, the British Red Cross joined the Order of St John, another Voluntary Aid Society that provided help to the aged, sick and injured, to form a Joint War Committee. Together, the two organizations built up a network of services both in France and at home. More ambulances were sent to France; more

THE BATH WAR QUILT

Regimental badges embroidered by patients at the War Hospital, Bath, as a form of therapy.

CHRISTMAS AT NETLEY HOSPITAL

In 1880, the British Red Cross asked permission from the War Office to train a small number of nurses at Netley in Hampshire, in preparation for times of emergency. Each trained nurse would then work in a military hospital for two years before using her skills for the Society. The first eight nurses to be trained were the forerunners of the many who were to work in service hospitals, such as that in Netley, in World War I.

hospitals and hospital trains were established; rest stations, recreation centres and hostels were set up. Owners of large houses and stately homes threw them open for the reception and care of convalescents, and hundreds of people volunteered their services.

Early in 1915, the War Office decided that nursing members of the VADs should be employed on contract in military hospitals. Later that year, female general service members were employed. As many as 15,000 worked at home and overseas as clerks, drivers, dispensers and X-ray assistants.

As fresh fronts opened in other parts of the world – in Italy and Gallipoli, in Salonika and Corfu, in the Balkans and Russia, in Palestine, Mesopotamia and Persia – the British Red Cross continued to offer relief and comfort. The Hague Regulations of 1907 had established the principle of relief parcels for prisoners of war, and throughout the war supplies were made up at Red Cross packing centres and despatched through the General Post Office. By November 1918, the Packing Department was despatching over 47,000 parcels a month.

An essential part of Red Cross services was the provision of hospital supplies and other materials. With the success of the appeal for funds, supplemented by gifts and by articles made by work parties, the Joint War Committee was able to supply items such as mobile units, motor launches, drugs and dressings, warm clothings, tents, linen, mosquito nets and collars and chains for dogs bringing the wounded in on sleighs from the North Russian Front. Hospitals at home and abroad were equipped, as were hospital ships and trains.

REST STATION, BOULOGNE

"I went to the Rest Station and found the VADs feeding a train… The men were haggard and dirty… nothing had been done for them since they left the dressing station…" Dame Katherine Furse.

Voluntary Aid Detachments

FROM 1909 THE WAR OFFICE placed a responsibility on the British Red Cross and the Order of St John to form Voluntary Aid Detachments (VADs) in every county in England to provide aid to the territorial medical service in times of war.

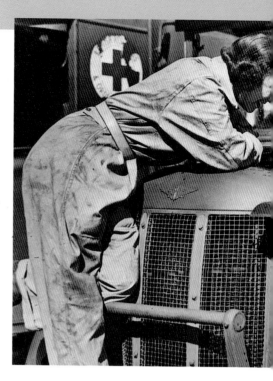

VAD SERVICE RECORD AND WATCH

A number of famous people, including Vera Brittain, Agatha Christie, E. M. Forster, John Masefield and Freya Stark, served as VADs during World War I. Agatha Christie claimed that she obtained her knowledge of poisons during her work as a dispenser.

DRIVERS IN WORLD WAR II

VADs served with the Forces in every theatre of war – as drivers, clerks, cooks, laboratory technicians and mechanics.

"SCRAMBLE"

When a hospital train is signalled, Red Cross ambulance drivers "scramble" to their vehicles at Etaples in France, near the front line during World War I.

1930s VAD CAMP

To qualify as VADs, women had to pass examinations in First Aid and Nursing (right); men had to pass First Aid only. These qualifications were renewed regularly.

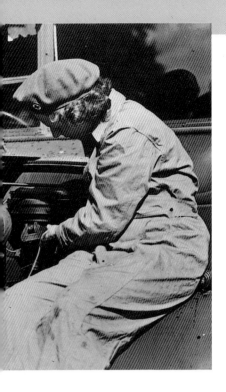

VADs began to help in hospitals and dispensaries during peacetime. The first public first aid duty was carried out at King George V's Coronation on 22 June 1911.

A few VADs gained their first experience of conflict in the Balkans during 1912–13 when the British Red Cross treated 16,358 patients from both sides. World War I saw the VADs fully mobilized and by 1918 there were over 90,000 British Red Cross VADs.

Being a VAD had a profound effect on many, particularly women who were freed from family and social constraints and were rewarded by the sense of vocation. After World War II, several joined the nursing profession and organizations such as the WRENS.

VADs were made up of men and women who voluntarily undertook a detailed training programme.

Although the VAD scheme was originally intended to provide voluntary aid in times of war, it was soon realized that practical experience was necessary and

CAPE AND BADGES

By World War II, VADs were transporting the wounded, manning dressing stations, and cooking and nursing in both military and auxiliary hospitals. This cape, the inside of which is covered by medals and mementoes given by both British and German soldiers, was worn by Jessie Crewe, who was clearly much admired by the men she nursed.

LETTER-WRITING, WORLD WAR II

One of the many tasks undertaken by VADs on behalf of the wounded was to write letters home.

THE INTER-WAR YEARS

WHEN WORLD WAR I ended in 1918, the British Red Cross entered a new phase in its history. As a founder member of the League of Red Cross Societies, the British Red Cross petitioned for and obtained a Supplemental Charter that extended its original objectives to include the improvement of health, the prevention of disease, and the mitigation of suffering throughout the world. This enabled the Society to embark on a programme of peacetime activities both at home and abroad.

HOP-PICKERS' DISPENSARIES

Hop-picking was a popular seasonal occupation during the 1920s and 30s. Whole families would move from the East End of London to Kent in the early autumn of each year and live in huts adjacent to the hop gardens. The nature of their work made them vulnerable to particular but treatable problems such as hopper's eye, hopper's rash and hopper's gout. The British Red Cross established dispensaries to meet the pickers' special needs. The first was opened in 1922; by 1929 there were seven dispensaries.

ROADSIDE FIRST AID POST

This first aid post on the London to Brighton road was staffed by members of Sussex branch. Similar first aid posts were located on major routes.

THE YARMOUTH DRESSING STATION

During October, the herring fleets of the North Sea came south. Fishing usually continued off the coast of East Anglia until the end of November. The very cold weather aggravated the severe cuts caused by the rough work and many wounds were infected by brine. The Norfolk branch of the British Red Cross responded to the needs of the men and women of the herring fishing fleet for treatment of these wounds by establishing dressing stations at Yarmouth and other posts on the east coast.

THE BLOOD TRANSFUSION SERVICE

In 1921, Percy Lane Oliver, Honorary Secretary of the Camberwell Division of the British Red Cross, received a telephone call

HOP-PICKERS

Clinic sessions such as this one for the children of hop-pickers at Hopfield in Kent played an important role in the improvement of health and prevention of disease in the hop-pickers and their families.

from King's College Hospital asking if he could find a volunteer to donate blood for a seriously ill patient. A suitable match was found and the patient's life was saved. As a result, Percy Oliver decided to form a panel of donors prepared to give blood to any hospital, day or night – the nation's first Transfusion Service was born. In the early months of 1939 the service responded to 5,333 requests. Even after the establishment of the National Health Service, the British Red Cross continued to provide help in an ancilliary specialist role until 1987.

HERRING GIRLS

The "fisher lassies" of the herring fleets were particularly grateful to receive treatment from the British Red Cross at the dressing stations established on the Norfolk coast.

ITALIAN-ETHIOPIAN WAR 1935–36

This brief but unequal struggle captured the shocked attention of people in the United Kingdom. When the Ethiopian Emperor Haile Selassie appealed for help to provide the medical services his country lacked, the British Red Cross responded by sending two ambulance units. The first was headed by Dr John Melly who had worked previously in Ethiopia. His colleague, Dr Kelly, led the second.

ADDIS ABABA, ETHIOPIA

Dr John Melly, who led the first British Red Cross ambulance unit to Ethiopia, was subsequently killed by sniper fire in 1936.

The doctors were confronted with an army in an appalling situation. Dr Empey, Melly's second in command, wrote about it later: "Besides the recent bomb or gunshot casualties, there were many with wounds (now festering and alive with larvae) sustained before the air raid. We also found tuberculosis, poliomyelitis, leprosy and dysentery. Having no native tradition of medicine, the people just didn't bother; but they were quick to appreciate the benefits of medical care."

Almost four months after setting up, a Red Cross camp was bombed and the operating unit destroyed. Despite this, the unit established a hospital in Addis Ababa. Shortly afterwards, John Melly was shot while treating a patient in the street. He died in the hospital on 5 May 1936.

WORLD WAR II 1939-45

THE WAR THAT BROKE OUT in 1939 had two significant differences from World War I. Firstly, only five countries – the Republic of Ireland, Spain, Sweden, Switzerland and Turkey – were neutral, and, secondly, the increased efficiency of weapons, aircraft and vehicles not only made the war one of continuous movement, but also resulted in a dramatic increase in civilian suffering.

I n the United Kingdom, the British Red Cross combined its work with the Order of St John to form the Joint War Organization. This ensured that personnel, fundraising and administration were organized as efficiently as possible. As a result, St John personnel also operated under the protection of the Red Cross emblem; both organizations are recognized as Voluntary Aid Societies under the Geneva Conventions.

AIR RAIDS

As Nazi forces assembled on the coasts of The Netherlands, Belgium and France for the invasion of England, the air raids began. After the airfields, London was the main target for heavy bombing in the early days, followed by the destruction of the city of Coventry in November 1940. Then came raids on Birmingham, Liverpool, Sheffield and Southampton. From 1941, the pattern spread to include the important ports of Bristol, Grimsby, Plymouth and Portsmouth and then, later, the cities of Bath, Canterbury, Exeter, Norwich and

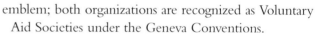

EVACUEES FROM FLYING BOMB ATTACKS

Long lines of evacuees, escaping from deadly flying bomb and rocket attacks, assembled at Paddington railway station in London with British Red Cross personnel as escorts.

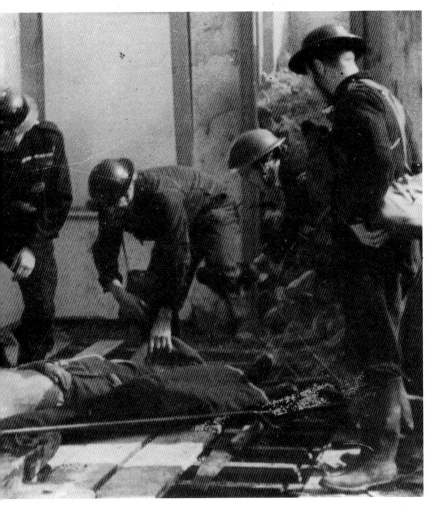

COMBINED FORCES

British Red Cross and Air Raid Precautions personnel often worked together, as seen here, to rescue the casualties of bomb attacks during World War II.

WORLD WAR II RED CROSS HELMET

This helmet is typical of those worn by British Red Cross personnel during the Blitz on Britain in World War II.

town of Weston-super-Mare. British Red Cross personnel served as part of the Civil Defence in first aid posts, casualty stations, shelters, sick bays, hostels, rest stations and mobile units throughout the country. British Red Cross ambulance drivers worked in all conditions to help the many civilians who were bombed out of their homes.

During the Blitz on London, 10,000 people a night were housed in tube shelters such as those at Holborn, Knightsbridge and Notting Hill Gate. Each had its own first aid post, manned by British Red Cross personnel. To ease the boredom of those in the shelters, Red Cross staff showed films and arranged concerts and games.

NEW HORRORS

As the war entered its final phase, new horrors threatened the battered population of London and the home counties: the first flying bomb attack was launched by the Germans in August 1944 and, a month later, the first rocket. Again, the British Red Cross provided assistance. At Chislehurst in Kent, a cave shelter that normally held 1,400 people was converted to accommodate nearly 10,000. The British Red Cross supplied mobile canteens to feed 1,000 people at a time.

COMFORT IN THE DARK HOURS

Members of the British Red Cross offered comfort as well as nursing care to civilians in bomb shelters such as the one below in the docklands of East London.

The Red Cross Parcel

ONLY ONE OF SEVERAL services provided for prisoners of war and civilian internees during both World Wars, the Red Cross Parcel is certainly the most famous and most affectionately remembered. The "Red Cross Lifeline", as it came to be known, brought food and personal items to keep recipients healthy and make their lives more bearable.

WWII POSTER

This poster was designed for an appeal made by the Duke of Gloucester's Red Cross and St John Fund, based at St James's Palace.

SPECIAL DELIVERY

Artificial legs for Wing Commander Douglas Bader were sent to him in his PoW camp in a Red Cross parcel.

Early in World War I, a Central Prisoners of War Committee was established by the Joint War Committee in order to regulate the contents, pack clothing and food parcels, and arrange their transportation for all those who might otherwise have nothing. In days when long-term storage of food was difficult, the Committee also established bakeries or bread bureaux in Switzerland

By the end of 1943, some 190,000 parcels were being hand-packed every week at 25 food parcel packing centres.

FOOD PARCEL CONTENTS

Parcel contents were chosen to give the best dietetic value and to supply foods lacking from prison camp diets.

POW "BLOWER"

This heating and cooking device made from tins contained in Red Cross food parcels was made by PoW Jack Stedman. Many PoWs made similar devices.

and Denmark to ensure each prisoner received the recommended levels of fresh bread or rusks every fortnight.

The Third Geneva Convention of 1929 provided for the humane treatment of prisoners of war, including the right of PoWs to receive individual parcels of food and clothing.

During World War II, the Prisoners of War Department of the Joint War Organization (JWO) was the accredited authority for their despatch. By May 1945, some 20 million food parcels containing biscuits, cheese, milk, chocolate, fruit or pudding, jam, margarine, two meats, sugar, tea, vegetables, vitamin supplements and cigarettes had been despatched. However, in the Far East in particular, delivery was patchy. Special Christmas parcels were despatched every August.

Besides food parcels, prisoners might also receive clothing parcels sent by their next of kin every three months, medical comforts such as hearing aids and spectacles, as well as books and sports equipment.

PARCEL STORE

British Red Cross parcels were sent by post to Lisbon, where they were stored before being shipped to Marseilles.

WORLD WAR II: WELFARE SUPPORT

WORLD WAR II BROUGHT an urgent need for auxiliary hospitals and convalescent homes for the wounded and for welfare support to returned prisoners of war and injured servicemen. Caring for children, whether evacuees or those whose parents were occupied with the war, was also a priority.

CHRISTMAS IN ST HELIER

The civilians on the Channel Islands receive some of the food parcels transported to them on the Vega.

In June 1940, at the request of the Ministry of Health, the British Red Cross and the Order of St John selected 234 country houses suitable for conversion into convalescent homes. Rest houses for Civil Defence workers and residential nurseries for children who were either delicate or the victims of air raids were established. Homes were also set up for Czech, Indian and Polish soldiers, for the Free French, for the Dutch Merchant Marine and to cope with those with special disabilities. There were also six homes for officers.

The first phase of the war saw the separation of parents from their children as the evacuation of the London area took place. Daily, rail termini were crowded with thousands of children, each labelled with a name and destination, waiting

> *"Ghost children who had no idea how to play have become real again and love their games."*
>
> SISTER IN CHARGE OF
> A RESIDENTIAL NURSERY

to be taken to unknown homes. Members of the Red Cross ensured that these bewildered children were taken to the right platform, given refreshments and comforted to help calm their fears.

CHANNEL ISLANDS

Through an agreement made in 1941, Channel Islanders were able to keep in touch with relatives through the Red Cross Message Service. After D-Day, as the German army retreated from the French

CHILDREN'S NURSERIES

Red Cross children's nurseries provided a safe and happy environment for those whose mothers were busy working for the war effort and whose fathers were serving in the Forces overseas.

RELAXING
ON THE TERRACE

*Convalescent homes for
wounded servicemen and
civilians were established
throughout Great Britain,
often in old country houses.*

coast, it became increasingly
difficult for them to supply the
blockaded islands, and both the
islanders and the German
garrisons faced starvation.
Negotiations between the International Committee of the Red Cross
and the German and British governments eventually resulted in
permission for relief supplies to be shipped under the auspices of the
Red Cross for the sole use of the islanders. The Red Cross charter
vessel, *Vega*, made several voyages to the islands between the end of
December 1944 and the Channel Islands' liberation on 9 May 1945.

OVERSEAS SUPPORT FOR THE FORCES

The first welfare officers to go overseas were two groups who, early in
1943, were posted to hospitals in Cairo and North Africa. They quickly
proved their value in boosting the morale of wounded servicemen by
providing emotional support and offering practical help, such as
writing regular progress reports
enabling patients and their families
to keep more closely in touch.
These welfare officers became
an established part of Red Cross
services in all Commissions.

DISPLACED PERSONS

As Allied armies advanced in
the theatres of war, they
were accompanied by
Red Cross relief teams.
British Red Cross teams
were the first into the
notorious concentration
camp at Belsen in April
1945, and remained
there for several months.

REPATRIATION OF POWS

*Welfare officers met returning prisoners
of war and wounded servicemen
arriving in England. Priority tasks
included handing out comforts bags,
tracing relatives and arranging relatives'
visits to those hospitalized.*

COMFORTS BAG

*Comforts bags contained the bare
essentials a wounded man or returned
PoW might need, such as a razor,
toothbrush and writing materials.*

Creativity in Captivity

EMBROIDERY AND OTHER HANDICRAFTS have often been
used as therapy for convalescent patients (see Bath War
Quilt, page 27). For the internees and prisoners of war of
World War II, they also provided a welcome break from
the boredom and privations of camp life.

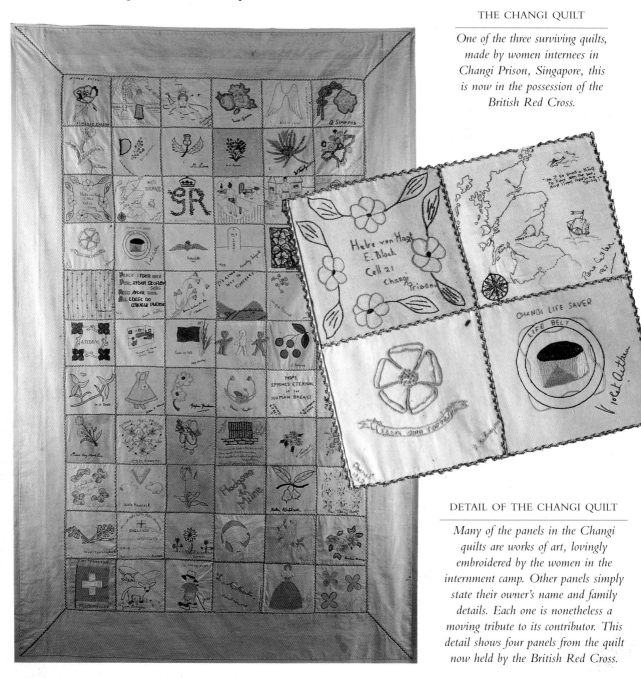

(see Bath War Quilt, page 27)

THE CHANGI QUILT

*One of the three surviving quilts,
made by women internees in
Changi Prison, Singapore, this
is now in the possession of the
British Red Cross.*

DETAIL OF THE CHANGI QUILT

*Many of the panels in the Changi
quilts are works of art, lovingly
embroidered by the women in the
internment camp. Other panels simply
state their owner's name and family
details. Each one is nonetheless a
moving tribute to its contributor. This
detail shows four panels from the quilt
now held by the British Red Cross.*

SIGNATURE PANEL

In Sime Road transit camp and later at Changi Prison, over 200 women, including six doctors, five matrons and 36 nurses of the Malayan Medical Service, wrote their names on this panel. The names were embroidered later by Deborah Gifford.

NOTHING WASTED

Many items were made from scraps of material or string. These string articles were made by women internees at Ilag Libenau Civilian Internment Camp in Germany.

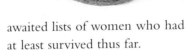

When the British garrison on the island of Singapore surrendered to the invading Japanese army early in 1942, many British service personnel and civilians were sent to internment camps. Apart from the many privations of camp life, one of the greatest problems was boredom. The idea of making large patchwork quilts formed of individually embroidered squares met with a ready response from a number of women internees.

Many of the men had no idea whether their wives and children were still alive. Each contributor was therefore asked to "put something of themselves" into the squares as well as embroidering her name. Later, when the Japanese camp commandant gave permission for the quilts to be given to the Military Hospital at Changi Prison, they provided long-awaited lists of women who had at least survived thus far.

Three quilts are known to exist. There was probably a fourth as the quilts were to be given to the Red Cross Societies of Australia, Canada, Great Britain and Japan when the war was over. One of the quilts now hangs in the British Red Cross museum at Barnett Hill in Surrey; two are in Australia. The location of the fourth quilt is not known.

GIFTS FOR THE POWS' CHILDREN

Middle East Army personnel made toys as presents for Far East PoWs to take home to their children on their release.

EMERGENCY RELIEF 1945-49

THE AFTERMATH OF WORLD WAR II had repercussions on British Red Cross work for many years. After five years of bitter conflict, the number of displaced and liberated people in need of basic supplies was huge. The relief effort was one that involved almost the entire Movement. However, the end of this widespread conflict did not preclude further bloodshed or distress. Soon there would be conflict in the Middle East and along the Indo-Pakistan border.

CIVILIAN RELIEF

A young Dutch refugee guards the family possessions at a British Red Cross/St John transit camp in 1945.

CANADIAN GIFT OF FOOD

Elderly people, young families and people with disabilities were hit particularly hard by post-war rationing. Parcels donated by the Canadian people in 1948, designed to supplement the ration provisions, were handed out to the most vulnerable by the British Red Cross.

AID TO BRITISH-BORN NATIONALS IN GERMANY AND AUSTRIA

In the aftermath of World War II, a great deal of civilian relief work was required in Germany and Austria. Food parcels were issued twice a month to 2,000 British, British-born or Dominion nationals in Germany and 800 to Austria. Much relief work was also done with the Austrian population, which suffered from every kind of shortage. Between 1946 and 1950, Red Cross workers covered hundreds of miles in all weathers and on appalling roads, distributing food to the needy. They set up many welfare centres and also acted as intermediaries for other Red Cross Societies.

HUNGARIAN REFUGEES

The British Red Cross assisted with the repatriation of thousands of Hungarian refugees during the winter and spring of 1945–46. Red Cross teams visited 80,000 refugees who had very little food and fuel. Many special projects were undertaken to assist the elderly and children, city dwellers and students.

PALESTINIAN REFUGEES

Following the birth of the state of Israel in 1948, a massive Palestinian refugee problem developed in Jordan with over 100,000 refugees in a country with a population of only 350,000. A British Red Cross headquarters was set up in Amman. Two field officers provided medical care in the camps and over £22,000 was spent on relief supplies.

INDO-PAKISTAN BORDER CONFLICT

In 1947, internal conflict in India and Pakistan caused millions of refugees to cross the Indo-Pakistan border, resulting in widespread disease and starvation. This was followed by flooding, which drowned many refugees, killed livestock and ruined crops. The British Red Cross supplied £20,000 of medicine, vitamins, clothing and blankets, as well as nursing assistance. The Indian Red Cross were given a donation of a dozen ambulances and medical equipment worth £25,000.

FLOODING IN GREAT BRITAIN

At home in the spring of 1947, disastrous floods occurred all over Britain, affecting 45,000 houses and 130,000 people. Relief work was undertaken in 30 counties, including emergency rescue work, the provision of temporary shelters and help for cases of distress. The Red Cross distributed approximately 26,400 cases of food and milk, in addition to sharing in the distribution of clothing, bedding and household commodities.

REHABILITATING THE CHILDREN

"...what absolutely magnificent work... the Red Cross teams [are] doing at Belsen... We have not heard enough of the heroism of the few English men and women who were first on the spot..."
DAME JANET VAUGHAN, MAY 1945

AUSTRALIAN FLOOD RELIEF

British Red Cross branches throughout the world were swift to respond when floods swept Britain in the spring of 1947.

Transporting the Wounded

"NO ONE CONCEIVED the restful comfort which they were to enjoy, and the effect on everyone brought down, in stimulating their recuperative powers, and affording complete easement from nervous strain and apprehension, was simply, even to me, marvellous." Major Cowan, medical officer on the *Mayflower* hospital ship, Sudan 1898.

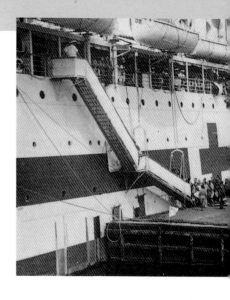

WORLD WAR II HOSPITAL SHIP

The distinctive white paint and red cross emblem protected hospital ships such as this from attack during World War II.

FIRE VICTIM SUPPORT UNIT

Specially designed mobile units such as the one above provide basic essentials such as clothes, money and a telephone to those whose homes have been destroyed by fire.

From the beginning the British Red Cross has made the provision of transport a priority. It recognized that establishing hospitals and training first aiders is of no use if the wounded or medical staff cannot get to the hospitals. The Society has always provided transport appropriate to both conditions and need. It used a steam launch on the Nile during the Egyptian Campaign of 1884;

THE LIGHT AMBULANCE, BOER WAR

Horse-drawn ambulances, such as this Light Ambulance, were not only slow but also painfully uncomfortable.

"THE WHITE TRAIN"

Hospital train No. 4, which was used in the Boer War of 1899–1902, was fondly known as The White Train.

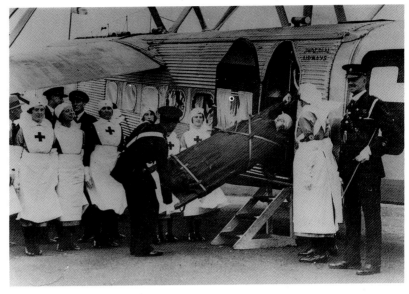

built the first hospital train in England and transported it to South Africa for service in the Boer War of 1899–1902; provided the first motorized vehicles to transport the wounded during World War I for an army still reliant on horse-drawn wagons; provided an air ambulance service in London and Manchester in the 1930s and organized Mobile Aid Units during World War II, which worked with the rescue squads caring for those injured in the blitz.

More recently, it donated a canoe to field officers of the Solomon Islands overseas branch in 1977 to enable them to run first aid and health care courses in schools and villages; and launched a pioneering mobile Fire Victim Support Unit in 1993, providing essential practical support to families in the aftermath of a fire in their homes.

AIR AMBULANCE TRANSPORT

In the early 1930s, Red Cross Air Ambulance Detachments were formed, based in Surrey and East Lancashire.

HOME AMBULANCE SERVICE

After World War I, the Joint Council of the Order of St John and the British Red Cross used the best surviving vehicles to provide a home ambulance service.

NORWICH RED CROSS AMBULANCE.

EMERGENCY RELIEF – 1950s

THE 1950S SAW THE END of the Allied occupation of West Germany and of the US occupation of Japan. It was the decade that witnessed the Korean War, the Suez Crisis, the Hungarian Uprising and conflict in newly independent Vietnam. There was a military coup in Pakistan and revolution in both Cuba and Iraq.

1958 GOLD MEDAL

This medal was presented to the British Red Cross by the Austrian Red Cross as thanks for the Society's help with Hungarian refugees.

KOREAN WAR

When war broke out between North and South Korea in 1950, Order of St John and British Red Cross welfare officers, who had proved so valuable during World War II that they had remained a vital part of the navy, army and air force hospitals at home and overseas, were sent to the British military hospitals and forward clearing stations. After the armistice in 1952, a British Red Cross team assisted in the repatriation of prisoners of war and a civilian relief team was despatched to help those civilians who had fled to the south from the conflict areas.

LYNTON AND LYNMOUTH FLOODS

The breaking of river banks as a result of torrential rain on the night of 15 August 1952 brought

1952 HARROW AND WEALDSTONE RAIL CRASH

Within 15 minutes of receiving a report of a terrible rail disaster at Harrow on 8 October, 26 men and women members of the Middlesex branch reported for duty.

1956 FOOD AID

Red Cross soup kitchens in Austria fed many of the refugees who fled from Hungary in November.

devastation to the popular North Devon holiday resorts of Lynton and Lynmouth. Somerset and Devon branches went into action immediately, setting up two fully-equipped rest centres and a sick bay. An ambulance toured Exmoor giving assistance, and branches throughout the country sent relief.

HUNGARIAN REVOLUTION

The British Red Cross was extensively involved in helping the thousands of refugees who fled from Hungary following the revolution in 1956. As well as contributing funds to support the work of the ICRC in Hungary itself, the Society also joined other national societies in helping the Austrian Red Cross to set up camps for the many refugees who crossed their border. Perhaps, though, the main achievement for the British Red Cross was organizing the airlift which brought to England over 7,500 refugees, who had been sleeping in the freezing open air while waiting for transport.

MAJOR EVENTS

- 1950 Continuing refugee crisis in Jordan
- 1950 Refugee crisis in Pakistan
- 1950 Mail train disaster, Republic of Ireland
- 1950 Colliery disaster, Cresswell, Derbyshire
- 1950–53 Korean War followed by refugee crisis
- 1950–51 Smallpox epidemic in Sussex
- 1952–55 Aid in resettlement camps in Malaya
- 1952 Floods in Lynton and Lynmouth, Devon
- 1952 Rail disaster, Harrow and Wealdstone, North London
- 1952 First aid support following Farnborough Air Display disaster, Hampshire
- 1953 East coast floods
- 1953 Earthquake in Cyprus
- 1955 Hurricane Janet in Barbados and the Windward Islands
- 1955 Severe floods in New South Wales and Queensland, Australia
- 1956 Uprising in Hungary
- 1956-59 Hungarian refugee crisis
- 1958 Cholera epidemic in Thailand
- 1958 Smallpox epidemic in Pakistan
- 1959 Aid for rehabilitation of victims of adulterated cooking oil disaster in Morocco

1953 EAST COAST

An onshore gale and a spring tide led to bad floods from the Humber to the Thames. British Red Cross members, with volunteers from St John Ambulance and the Women's Royal Voluntary Service, provided vital support.

EMERGENCY RELIEF – 1960s

WITH INCREASINGLY WIDESPREAD ACCESS to news reports on television, the public of the 1960s became more aware of world events, such as the building of the Berlin Wall, the Cuban missile crisis, the cultural revolution in China, the six-day Arab-Israeli War, and the beginning of what were termed "the Troubles" in Northern Ireland.

1966 VILLAGE OF ABERFAN, WALES

On 19 October, a coal tip collapsed, smothering a school. The British Red Cross rushed vital supplies to the scene. Members gave unstinting help in the mortuary and to the bereaved.

1961 MODEL BOAT FROM TRISTAN DA CUNHA

Islanders, evacuated to the U.K. when the island's volcano erupted, made this gift.

MOROCCO

In March 1960, an earthquake virtually destroyed the town of Agadir in Morocco, causing 15,000 casualties and severely disrupting medical facilities. The British Red Cross immediately sent a team of specialists and nurses to help care for the most seriously injured and contributed to the rebuilding and re-equipping of the general hospital. In a large-scale operation, the British Red Cross also contributed tents, blankets, camp-beds, folding cots and mattresses for the homeless and a fully equipped field kitchen.

HURRICANE HATTIE

For British Honduras (now Belize), 31 October 1961 brought widespread destruction in the shape of Hurricane Hattie and the subsequent tidal wave. Even though many of their own homes were in ruins, members of the British Honduras branch of the British Red Cross brought aid to the victims and opened an emergency feeding centre in Belize City, the then capital. In accordance with pre-arranged plans, the Jamaican branch of the British Red Cross mobilized and despatched relief

1961 WRECKAGE OF HURRICANE HATTIE

Within hours of the winds abating, members of the British Honduras branch battled through the floods to bring aid to the victims.

supplies on behalf of headquarters in London. Field workers were sent out from England to lend their expertise to the massive task of feeding, clothing, sheltering and rehabilitating the victims.

IRANIAN EARTHQUAKE

On 1 September 1962, a severe earthquake hit Iran, destroying many villages. The devastation was mostly in remote mountain districts and it was often necessary to climb over rocky tracks to reach the survivors. The nearest hospital was 60 miles away. In the first-ever television charity appeal, Richard Dimbleby requested urgent funds, raising an unprecedented £407,501. Although the first consignment of bandages, blankets and tents was welcome, the need to provide adequate housing before the onset of winter was given top priority. Most of the Society's funds were spent on erecting prefabricated houses for 75,000 homeless people. Eight villages were completely rebuilt with money provided by the British Red Cross. In addition, blankets were transported to the stricken area, to be made into chadors for the women.

YEMEN

As brutal conflict raged between North and South Yemen in 1963, the British Red Cross sent two doctors and a medical orderly to be seconded to the ICRC. Their first headquarters and dispensary was a cave where the injured queued for treatment. Later the team travelled to other parts of the interior and worked in the ICRC's field hospital which had been specially flown in from Switzerland and weighed just 3.5 tons. Within weeks, the hospital treated over 200 in-patients and 1,000 out-patients.

THE DEC

In 1966, the Society agreed to co-operate with five other major charities in Britain to form the Disasters Emergency Committee to launch free television appeals following major overseas disasters. The DEC still exists and today comprises seven leading UK agencies.

MAJOR EVENTS

- 1960 Earthquakes in Morocco and Chile
- 1960 Cyclones in Mauritius
- 1960 Hurricane Donna in the West Indies
- 1960 Floods in Southern England and Wales
- 1961 Hurricane Hattie in British Honduras
- 1961–65 Conflict in Rwanda; refugees in Uganda
- 1962 Earthquake in Iran
- 1962–65 Famine in Kenya
- 1963–69 Conflict in the Yemen
- 1963 Freeze in England and Wales
- 1964 Conflict in Cyprus
- 1965-69 Conflict in Vietnam
- 1965 Conflict in India and Pakistan
- 1965 Cyclone in Pakistan
- 1966 Earthquakes in Eastern Turkey
- 1966-67 Famine in India
- 1966 Landslip, Aberfan, Wales
- 1967-69 Conflict in Nigeria
- 1968 Earthquakes in Italy and Iran
- 1968 Rail disaster, Hixon, Northumbria
- 1969 Floods in Tunisia and Algeria
- 1969 Drought in Somalia

1962 IRANIAN HOMELESS

The earthquake that struck Iran left many families homeless.

EMERGENCY RELIEF — 1970s

THE DECADE that saw the end of the Vietnam War and the Camp David agreement on peace in the Middle East was also witness to brutal and bitter conflicts throughout the world — from military coups in Argentina and Chile and civil war in Angola to the Soviet invasion of Afghanistan and the Islamic revolution in Iran.

1970 PLAQUE FROM TURKISH RED CRESCENT

This was given to the British Red Cross in thanks for aid in the 1970 earthquake.

HAMPSTEAD FLOOD VICTIMS

August 1975 brought severe flooding to the north London suburb of Hampstead. The local British Red Cross centre opened its doors for nearly a week, providing refuge for many elderly people, young families and students whose homes were damaged.

NEW FOREST FIRE

In the summer of 1976, fire swept across the New Forest threatening to engulf St Leonard's hospital. Within 20 minutes of the news, the first team of British Red Cross branch members arrived at the hospital to help evacuate 360 elderly people. Three hundred holidaymakers from a nearby caravan site were also evacuated. Volunteers prepared the rest centre for the evacuees, and continued working for several days, particularly making up emergency bed packs for the elderly people returning to the hospital.

NORWICH CITY FOOTBALL VIOLENCE

Thirty-six casualties, including one Red Cross official, were treated by British Red Cross volunteers during serious crowd disturbances at a football match between Norwich City and Manchester United at the end of the

1972 CORN DISTRIBUTION, CHITTAGONG

Bangladesh was a major recipient of Red Cross aid in the 1970s.

1976 AID TO ITALY

The Red Cross tent village set up in Gemona, Italy after the earthquake.

MAJOR EVENTS

- 1970 Floods in Romania
- 1970 Earthquakes in Turkey and Peru
- 1970 Cyclone in East Pakistan
- 1970 Civil war in Jordan
- 1970-79 Conflict in South Vietnam and Cambodia
- 1971 Conflicts in India and Pakistan
- 1972 Asian refugees from Uganda arrive in Britain
- 1972 Relief to Bangladesh
- 1972 Earthquake in Nicaragua
- 1973 Floods in Pakistan
- 1973 Conflict in the Middle East
- 1973–79 Natural and man-made disasters lead to emergency in Sahelian zone and Ethiopia
- 1974 Aid to victims of conflict in Cyprus
- 1974 Hurricane Fifi in Honduras
- 1974 Floods in Bangladesh
- 1975 Underground crash, Moorgate, London
- 1975-77 Conflict in the Lebanon and Angola
- 1976 Earthquakes in Guatemala, Italy and Turkey
- 1977 Two cyclones and tidal waves in India
- 1978 Refugees from Burma in Bangladesh
- 1979 Hurricane David in Dominica
- 1979 Civil war in Nicaragua

football season in 1977. John Bond, manager of Norwich City, later praised the volunteers: "It's invaluable to have voluntary trained people in such situations – without them we would have been lost."

VIETNAMESE REFUGEES

For Vietnamese refugees fleeing the war in their homeland, some of their first comforts on arrival in the United Kingdom in 1976 were provided by the British Red Cross. Teams of volunteers met the refugees at Stansted airport and accompanied them to the reception centres. A British Red Cross medical centre at Sopley Camp in Hampshire run by volunteers provided 24-hour cover for six weeks. Once the refugees left the reception centres, volunteers at local branches again lent a helping hand.

CYCLONES IN INDIA

In November 1977, two cyclones and tidal waves hit the states of Tamil Nadu and Andhra Pradesha, killing over 25,000 people and leaving two million homeless. The Indian Red Cross distributed emergency relief while the British Red Cross donated £25,000 and sent two plane-loads of Land Rovers and radio sets.

1977 FIRST AID FOR FOOTBALL FANS

Society members care for victims of crowd violence at Carrow Road, Norwich City's football ground.

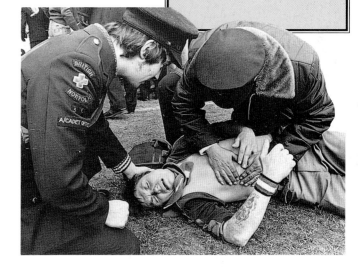

Transporting Supplies

A VITAL PART of emergency relief work is, and always has been, transporting supplies to the stricken area. Whenever disaster strikes, images of life-saving aid reaching the afflicted people fill our newspapers and television screens. Whether dropped from a Hercules transport plane or delivered in a convoy, this aid brings hope and relief.

£10 could buy any of the following:
19 litres of vegetable oil
6,000 water purifying tablets, each making one litre of clean water • 5 blood bags
50 kilos of rice • 85 kilos of flour • 3 blankets
30 kilos of sugar • 1 set of cooking pots

LAND TRANSPORT

Convoys of Red Cross aid often travel through hostile territory, relying on the protective powers of the emblem.

Transporting aid requires detailed planning and efficiency. These skills were established from the outset. During the Franco-Prussian War of 1870–71, 12,000 bales of essential supplies such as linen, clothing and surgical instruments, weighing four tons each, were despatched every day over a period of 188 days without interruption. Such was the efficiency of the operation that when a request came for 250 iron bedsteads for a hospital at Pont-à-Mousson in northern France, they arrived just 48 hours later!

During World War I, the list of goods available from the British Red Cross stores included such unlikely items as corkscrews, sewing machines, basting spoons and deck chairs. In the two weeks following the D-Day landings in June 1944, the stores department

TRANSPORTING BY SEA

A cargo of aid is loaded on to a ship chartered by the British Red Cross.

AIR AID

*Land Rovers and supplies are often
flown in to disaster areas.*

issued over five million cigarettes,
53,500 razor blades, 29,000 pairs
of pyjamas, 19,000 handkerchiefs
and 17,500 packets of stationery.
Today, the British Red Cross
supplies aid after natural
disasters as directed by the
International Federation in
Geneva, which ensures that
relief effort is not duplicated and
that aid is stored and distributed
according to the principles of
neutrality and impartiality.
Whatever the disaster, the Society
ensures that the right aid reaches
the right people in the shortest
time and at the best possible cost.

HUMAN TRANSPORTATION

*Medical supplies being carried on foot
in Mozambique.*

EMERGENCY RELIEF – 1980S

THE 1980S WILL BE REMEMBERED for the worldwide awareness of the catastrophic famine in Ethiopia, the Falklands War, and increased tension in the Middle East, with the start of the Iran-Iraq War, the Israeli invasion of the Lebanon and the US invasion of Libya. The decade ended with the dismantling of the Berlin Wall and the end of the Cold War, and the Tiananmen Square massacre in China.

1988 LOCKERBIE, SCOTLAND

Members provided practical and emotional support to rescuers and relatives following the air disaster in December.

1985 PILATUS PLANE

This model was made from butter oil cans by a refugee at an Ethiopian feeding centre.

CAMBODIA (KAMPUCHEA) AND THAILAND

By 1980, bitter internal conflict in Cambodia and the resulting famine led the ICRC, in conjunction with UNICEF, and supported by financial contributions from national societies, to embark on the largest aid programme in its history to provide food and medical supplies within the country. Hundreds of thousands of refugees were spilling over the border into Thailand. The Red Cross recruited a team of 100 doctors and nurses from around the world to treat the sick. In March 1980, the British Red Cross had 17 medical staff in Thailand; by the end of the year, 55 British delegates formed one of the largest Red Cross medical teams in the field. In 1993/4, the Society was greatly involved in a programme to return refugees to Cambodia.

1987 THE HERALD OF FREE ENTERPRISE

Some 200 members helped survivors and relatives when this ferry sank off Zeebrugge.

ETHIOPIA AND SUDAN

The greatest disaster to disturb the world's conscience in the 1980s was the appalling famine in Africa, from Angola to Mauritania. Attention focused on Ethiopia. In July 1984, the Disasters Emergency Committee (see page 47) launched an appeal which raised £19.4 million in three months, a record response at the time. The British Red Cross later launched its own appeal. The scale of the famine necessitated

1980-9 FAMINE IN AFRICA

An Angolan child receives much-needed food.

huge commitments of aid – some 65,000 tons of food per month in 1985. The British Red Cross gave substantial funds and many shipments of wheat, sugar, edible oils and other supplies. The British Red Cross also played an increasingly important role in relief operations in Sudan, where the problems caused by famine were compounded by the massive influx of thousands of destitute refugees from neighbouring countries such as Chad and Ethiopia. The British Red Cross began a five-year programme of support involving the provision of funds and personnel to help the Sudanese Red Crescent develop its strength and capability.

PIPER ALPHA

On 6 July 1988, the Piper Alpha oil installation in the North Sea was racked by an explosion. Only 65 of the 232 people on the rig survived. British Red Cross members staffed an emergency reception centre close to Aberdeen airport and provided compassionate care for the distressed relatives. Red Cross escorts accompanied those who could not face the journey home alone. For two weeks after the tragedy, members manned a telephone hotline 24 hours a day.

MAJOR EVENTS

- 1980–89 Vietnamese refugees in Hong Kong
- 1980–81 Earthquakes in Algeria and Italy and aftermath
- 1980–89 Famine in Africa, particularly in Ethiopia and Sudan
- 1980 Conflict in Afghanistan
- 1980–82 Cambodian refugees in Thailand
- 1980 Renewed conflict in the Lebanon
- 1981 Civil war in El Salvador
- 1981 Outbreak of Iran-Iraq War
- 1981 Two earthquakes in Italy
- 1982 Falklands War
- 1985 Cyclone and tidal wave in Bangladesh
- 1985 Volcanic eruption in Colombia
- 1987 Capsize of passenger ferry, Zeebrugge, Holland
- 1987 Conflict in Mozambique
- 1987 Devastating storms in southern England
- 1988 Oil rig disaster, North Sea
- 1988 Air disaster, Lockerbie, Scotland
- 1988 Hurricanes in the Caribbean and Nicaragua
- 1988 Earthquake in Armenia
- 1989 Plane crash on M1 motorway, West Midlands
- 1989 Football stadium tragedy, Hillsborough, Yorkshire
- 1989 Hurricane Hugo in the Caribbean

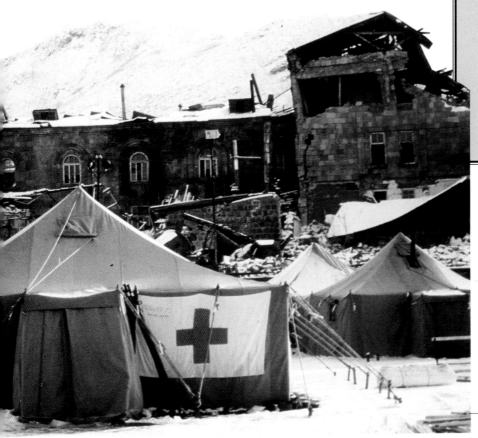

1988 ARMENIAN RELIEF

The Red Cross directed relief for the victims of the Armenian earthquake from a tent in the midst of the ruins of Spitak.

EMERGENCY RELIEF – 1990s

CONFLICT AND ITS AFTERMATH have dominated the 1990s. The decade began with a bitter and brutal civil war in Liberia and the Iraqi invasion of Kuwait. The Gulf War of 1991 was soon followed by civil war in Yugoslavia. Famine and civil war in Somalia caused the deaths of thousands, while the slaughter in Rwanda brought scenes of unimaginable horror.

1991-5 FORMER YUGOSLAVIA

The red cross emblem identifies the battle-scarred hospital at Osijek, Croatia.

1991 KURDISH VICTIMS

Amongst the many refugees fleeing Iraq, the elderly, the sick and children were particularly vulnerable.

GULF WAR AFTERMATH

With the cessation of hostilities in the Gulf War in 1991, for which the Society had organized a massive programme of care for the expected casualties, world attention focused on the plight of refugees fleeing from Iraq to neighbouring Iran and Turkey. In the first six months of the year, some 1.5 million people, about half of them children, made the treacherous journey across the borders in weather where temperatures plummeted each night. In the camps where thousands settled, many died of exposure or from disease caused by the lack of basic sanitation.

The British Red Cross chartered 14 aircraft to fly out aid including blankets, tents, food and medical supplies worth over £1.4 million. In September, 18 trucks were sent to assist the Iranian Red Crescent with the supply operation and £1 million was given to support a United Nations operation to provide 700,000 Kurdish refugees with shelters.

SOMALIA

By the summer of 1992, some 4,000 people were dying every day in Somalia, a country ravaged by civil war and famine. For a nation of just seven million citizens, this represented a catastrophe of unimaginable proportions. Refugees flooded across the border with Kenya into Red Cross camps. The largest of these, Utange, housed some 18,000 refugees, while another 15,000 lodged outside. The ICRC

1994 TANZANIAN REFUGEE RECEPTION CENTRE

Many Rwandans fled to camps in surrounding countries.

sustained a massive medical and relief operation within Somalia, the largest undertaken anywhere in the world since World War II. British Red Cross Director General Mike Whitlam and International Director Geoffrey Dennis visited the area to assess priorities. The Society sent vital aid including plastic sheeting, trucks and medical supplies. It also funded all the supplies and necessary equipment for 60 of the 900 kitchens feeding 1.5 million people daily.

RWANDA

The Rwanda emergency in 1994 demanded the largest relief operation by the International Red Cross. Almost a million people are estimated to have died as a result of widespread massacres during the first four months of the fighting. Of a population of seven million, two million people were displaced within Rwanda, and a further two million fled to Tanzania, Zaire, Burundi and Uganda. In the first six months, the British Red Cross sent 55 delegates and chartered 20 relief flights, carrying blankets, plastic sheeting, water containers, medical supplies, tents, vehicles, water tanks and generators.

FORMER YUGOSLAVIA

Caught in the most serious conflict in Europe since World War II, thousands of people in former Yugoslavia have been killed or made homeless. At one point the Red Cross was providing half the total aid. In 1993 alone, the ICRC visited over 16,000 detainees, handled over four million messages, supplied 190 medical facilities and distributed relief supplies to some one million people. The British Red Cross is one of many national societies participating in the Federation's enormous relief programme for 1.5 million people in Croatia, Serbia/Montenegro, Macedonia and Slovenia, distributing food, hygiene parcels, infant care parcels and medical supplies and running a social welfare programme for psychologically traumatized persons, refugees and displaced people.

MAJOR EVENTS

- 1990 Aid to Romania
- 1990 Famine in Ethiopia and Sudan
- 1990 Earthquake in Iran
- 1990 Eight typhoons in China
- 1990 Conflict in Sri Lanka, Liberia, the Middle East and Somalia
- 1990 Exodus from Iraq following invasion of Kuwait
- 1991 Gulf War: Kurdish refugees and civilian crisis in Iraq
- 1991 Conflict, drought and famine in the Horn of Africa
- 1991 Floods in China
- 1991-95 Conflict in former Yugoslavia
- 1991 Crisis in Albania and the former Soviet Union
- 1991 Cyclone in Bangladesh
- 1991 Earthquake and floods in war-torn Afghanistan
- 1992 Floods in Pakistan
- 1992 Repatriation of refugees to Cambodia, Afghanistan and Vietnam
- 1993 Floods and landslides in India, Nepal and Bangladesh
- 1993 Earthquake in central India
- 1993 Floods in Wales
- 1993-94 Conflicts in Angola, Liberia and Rwanda
- 1994 Floods in Scotland
- 1995 Earthquake in Japan

COMFORTING FIRE VICTIMS

In the UK, the Fire Victim Support Unit provides practical and emotional support to those whose homes have been damaged or destroyed.

Delegates Abroad

SENDING SKILLED PERSONNEL to aid relief operations overseas is a key aspect of the Society's work and delegates undertaking that work follow in a great tradition. Two months after the Society's foundation in 1870 (see pages 10–11), 62 surgeons, 16 nurses and 32 agents were sent abroad to care for the victims of the Franco-Prussian War. Despite the dangers, many others were willing to go.

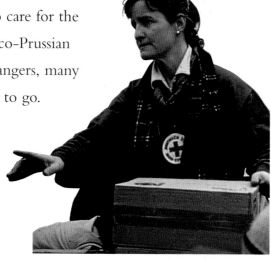

FORMER
YUGOSLAVIA

Nurse Annie Sewell organizes the distribution of medical supplies in 1994.

Sometimes, in the conflicts that have followed, British Red Cross medical personnel alone provided relief from suffering. During the Russo-Turkish war of 1877–78, one correspondent for the *Daily Telegraph* wrote: "for an army of 40,000 men, there is only one ambulance attended by two doctors, who have dressed

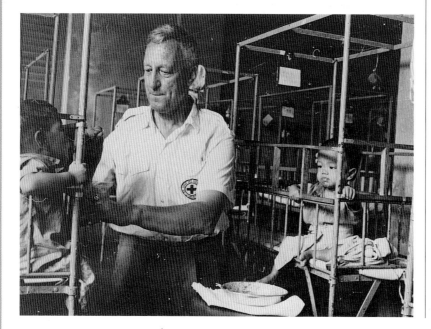

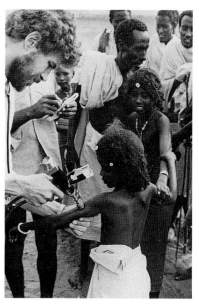

VIETNAM

Arnold Plummer, medical assistant, with two of the 1,900 patients in 1968 at the Cu Lao Giang orphanage, Mekong.

ETHIOPIA

Dr Jonathan Michael, medical team leader, carries out an emergency smallpox vaccination's in 1974.

SUDAN

Dr Elizabeth Archer in 1982 caring for refugees escaping the conflict in Chad.

hundreds of wounds in the last few days... this solitary ambulance... was sent out by the English Red Cross Society". Shortly after, one of these doctors, Francis Meyrick, died of exhaustion, aged 22.

DELEGATES TODAY

Today's delegates travel wherever they are needed to provide care for people suffering as a result of conflict or natural disaster. They are doctors, nurses, mechanics, technicians; their work is based on the fundamental principles of neutrality, impartiality and humanity (see pages 8–9).

THAILAND

Jenny Deakin, one of the British Red Cross nurses who cared for thousands of refugees who fled across the border in 1979 from Cambodia into Thailand.

TANZANIA

Sheila Wilson, head of relief in the camp in Benaco, Tanzania, for refugees of the conflict in Rwanda, 1994.

WHERE THE SOCIETY IS WORKING TODAY

THE BRITISH RED CROSS contributes both expertise and materials to many areas of the world. The map shows the location of delegates and projects as at December 1994, including Rwanda, the largest operation in the 1990s in which the British Red Cross has participated. It also includes those countries where the International Tracing and Message Service is most heavily involved.

OVERSEAS WORK

The Society today is most involved in Eastern Europe, Africa and the Asian Pacific region. The main focus of this work is in logistics, healthcare, water sanitation and refugees.

*Former Yugoslavia includes Bosnia, Croatia, Serbia and Slovenia

FORMER YUGOSLAVIA★

British Red Cross teams have worked both in the war zones and with refugees and displaced people.

AFGHANISTAN

The population of Kabul has endured constant, indiscriminate shelling.

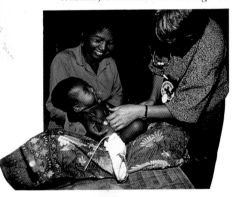

CAMBODIA

Nurses tend a young child in a country where land-mines from the conflict maim civilians.

Tajikistan

Afghanistan

Pakistan

Nepal

Hong Kong

Bangladesh

Myanmar

Laos

India

Thailand

Cambodia

Sri Lanka

Malaysia

RWANDA

Some 100,000 children have been orphaned or separated from their parents.

TYPICAL DISASTER RESPONSE TIME

WHEN DISASTER STRIKES, the unique network of the Red Cross and Red Crescent Societies ensures that the right aid reaches those most in need as quickly and efficiently as possible. The chart, see right, details the three phases through which the response to a disaster might go from the point of view of the British Red Cross.

At the site of a major disaster, the International Federation's Rapid Response Team (RRT) and the local society investigate to assess and prioritize immediate needs. They decide whether or what assistance is required. The RRT have a list of national societies with teams of people and units of emergency equipment which can be rushed to the scene of a disaster immediately. The British Red Cross has offered an emergency medical team, a small-scale water supply unit, an airport logistics team, and a sanitation unit. The ICRC and or the Federation will request the use of one or more of these teams from the national societies concerned and the relevant aid and personnel will be on site within 24-48 hours of the disaster. As the situation develops, the on-site teams will request further supplies as necessary. These appeals will be transmitted via the Federation to all national societies. Finally, once the initial priorities have been met, the work of rehabilitating those affected takes over for as long as is required.

EMERGENCY RESPONSE PHASES

PHASE ONE

- Disaster strikes

- Federation mobilize a rapid response team made up of 3-4 specialists; often one is from the British Red Cross

- In conjunction with the local national society, the rapid response team assesses priority needs and matches these against a checklist of available aid and expertise from national societies.

- 24-48 hours later, in response to a request from the Federation, the British Red Cross despatches its medical emergency mobile team who are fully equipped to deal with the priority needs in the immediate aftermath of disaster.

PHASE TWO

- Teams at the disaster site monitor the situation and appeal through the Federation for aid and equipment still required.

- An appeal is sent to all national societies, and through them to national governments, the European Union and private donors, who indicate their ability to respond.

- The aid is delivered to the teams at the disaster site for as long as required.

- Personnel are despatched, typically medical, logistics, drivers, engineers and project managers.

PHASE THREE

- The longer-term needs of those affected by the disaster are monitored; programmes for their rehabilitation are initiated and developed in conjunction with the local national society.

ASSESSING NEEDS

Assessing the priority needs following a major disaster is a key stage of effective disaster response.

3

WORK
IN THE
COMMUNITY

The British Red Cross Society plays an
important role in caring for people in crisis
within the local community. It does this in
many ways: from setting up first aid posts
at public events to providing services for people
in need in their own homes. This chapter
illustrates the importance of specialized,
up-to-date training, backed up by practical
information found in the Society's publications.
The commitment of Red Cross Youth and
Juniors and the tireless work of the Tracing
Service are also celebrated.

TRAINING

"THIS WOULD SEEM to be the inception of a movement which is likely to be of great service in giving first aid in cases of National disaster and to afford valuable training of a practical character to members of Voluntary Aid organizations... If established it cannot fail to be of great benefit to the community." *British Medical Journal*, 1913, on the beginning of formal training of VADs.

TRAINING PIONEERS

VADs on a field day in Trumpington, Cambridge, in 1912 practise first aid.

With the formation of Voluntary Aid Detachments in 1909 came the first organized training schemes for the British Red Cross. Training was considered vital if VADs were to be effective in providing support to the territorial medical services. All members of the very first detachments had to be trained in first aid and nursing to War Office standards. Training was also provided in making use of local resources to make stretchers, find transport and for converting local buildings into "shelters" and rest stations for the sick and wounded.

In 1911, the War Office gave permission for the Society to grant its own certificates in first aid and nursing, and the first Proficiency badge was introduced. By the beginning of World War I, every VAD had to have successfully completed a Red Cross first aid course; all women had to have a further certificate in Red Cross nursing. By this date, the range of courses included hygiene and sanitation; a certificate in cookery was added two years later. Each of the detachments was inspected every year to ensure its training was up to date, and all members were obliged to renew their certificates if they wished to remain in the detachment.

AIR RAID PRECAUTIONS TRAINING

The XIIth International Conference of 1925 declared it to be the duty of national societies to study methods of protection

AIR RAID PRECAUTIONS TRAINING

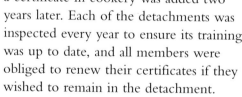

The British Red Cross invested much time and energy training its personnel in protecting and treating civilians in the event of aerial warfare.

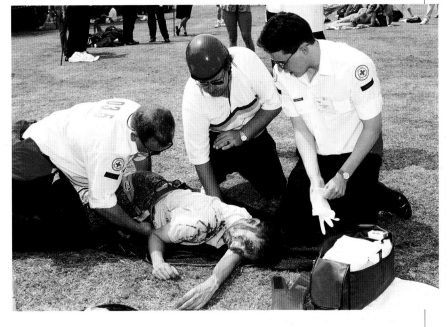

GAS DECONTAMINATION SQUAD

With the very real threat of gas attack looming in the 1930s, training in coping with the aftermath was a top priority.

and treatment of soldiers and civilians against the possible effects of aerial warfare. The British Red Cross, therefore, began training its detachments and had issued 6,789 certificates by the end of 1935. It even published its own manual, *First Aid in Chemical Warfare*. With the threat of war looming, the Society assisted the government and local authorities with arrangements for the protection of the public against the effects of air attack. In October 1935, 35 male and female officers attended a course of instruction at the Anti-Gas Wing at Winterbourne Gunner – the first time that women were admitted as students of a military academy.

TRAINING TODAY

Today the Society provides a range of training courses for its own volunteers and for members of the public. In recent years, the need for everyone to have some first aid knowledge has become increasingly apparent; first aid knowledge can save lives. The British Red Cross provides courses to suit every need – from short two-hour courses in life-saving to the full Standard First Aid course, First Aid at Work training and First Aid for Motorists. As well as running courses in nursing and welfare, the British Red Cross also provides specialized training for child minders, pre-school play groups and babysitters and in subjects including crisis care and international humanitarian law.

As with the VADs in 1909, the British Red Cross still regards the proper training of its members as vital if the Society is to provide efficient and effective support to the statutory services. Regular training exercises are organized to ensure that this support is both immediate and effective.

EUROPEAN FIRST AID COMPETITION

Maintaining high standards of first aid knowledge within its own membership is a priority for the British Red Cross. In 1994, the British team was victorious for the third time in four years at the annual European First Aid Competition which promotes excellence in first aid practice.

FIRST AID AT WORK TRAINING

In 1993, nearly 55,000 people learned how to cope with an accident in the workplace as a result of attending a British Red Cross course. Over 160,000 people were trained in first aid overall.

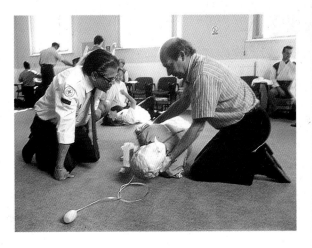

Books

IF THE WRITTEN WORD played a major part in the beginnings of the Red Cross in Henry Dunant's recollections of Solferino (see pages 6–7), it now plays an increasingly important role in ensuring that both the story of the Movement and practical information are readily available to the public. Training materials and reference books are the main publications, each regularly updated to incorporate new practices or new areas of concern.

SIR JAMES AND LADY CANTLIE

Sir James Cantlie wrote the very first, highly successful First Aid Manual *for the British Red Cross in 1911.*

CASUALTY FAKING

Faking casualties is an essential part of training; the more realistic the scenarios, the better the training. This title was published in 1949.

British Red Cross publications through the years have been diverse, reflecting the changing emphasis of the Society. Perhaps the best-known is the *First Aid Manual*. As early as 1911, Sir James Cantlie had written the first of these, along with the *Red Cross Nursing Manual* and the *Red Cross Training Manual*. Since that date, the *First Aid Manual* has been constantly revised and updated, incorporating advances in knowledge and procedures. For example, the third edition, published in 1926, included an appendix on chemical warfare, in recognition of the increasing threat of such weapons being used in conflict. Today's *First Aid Manual*, produced in conjunction with the St John Ambulance Association and the St Andrew's Ambulance Association, is one of the foremost such reference books available. A more recent publication is *First Aid for Children Fast*, a quick-reference book for parents and those who look after children.

First aid knowledge, however, is not the only concern of the British Red Cross today. Other publications include the *Multi-Lingual Phrasebook*, which gives

FIRST AID MANUAL

First written in 1911 by Sir James Cantlie, the First Aid
Manual *has become an established work of reference and
is now in its sixth edition.*

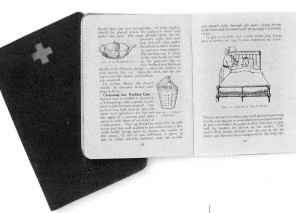

immediate translations of basic
medical questions in 28 languages;
handbooks for babysitters, which
detail the rights and responsibilities
of parents and babysitters in the
short-term care of young children;
and the *Disaster Appeal Scheme*, a
blueprint for local authorities that
might need to set up an appeal
following a disaster in their area.
The Society continually publishes
new titles to accompany its ever-
expanding training programme.

TRAINING MANUALS

*Topics from health and hygiene
to nursing were just some of
those covered by early Red
Cross manuals. Today's
publications include* First
Aid for Children Fast *and*
A Handbook for Babysitters
*and reflect the Society's growing
areas of interest and influence.*

RED CROSS YOUTH AND JUNIORS

ON THE PROPOSAL in 1921 to form a Junior Red Cross movement Sir Phillip Gibbs, war correspondent, wrote: "It seems to me the most beautiful experiment in the re-shaping of human society which has happened since the world went mad in 1914... It is a great adventure of youth which may lead to the discovery of new worlds... united by friendly understanding, compassion for the inevitable suffering of the human family and helpful service to one another."

GLAMORGAN BRANCH SWIMMING CLUB

The swimming club attached to the Glamorgan branch was in existence two years before Juniors were given official recognition. It was the first branch to enrol female Junior members.

JUNIOR RED CROSS DRILL AND RESCUE TRAINING

In the 1960s, young members could train in a wide range of subjects including drill and rescue, as here. Other training included first aid, nursing, infant and child care, hygiene, fire protection, messenger work and home mechanics.

Although the British Red Cross was founded in 1870, the Junior Red Cross movement did not become firmly established in this country for another 50 years. The British Red Cross was by no means the first national society to realize the potential of young people to undertake its work: there was a young persons' movement in Bulgaria as early as 1885 and in 1896 the Spanish Red Cross began admitting school children into its membership. However, although the British Junior Movement was officially founded in 1924, it is clear that young people were very active in support of the Society during World War I. One of children's main tasks then was to collect sphagnum moss from the moors. The moss contains iodine and has valuable absorbent and antiseptic qualities; it was widely used by the Society to make dressings for the wounded. In 1918 alone, nearly two million such dressings were supplied by the British Red Cross.

From the outset, there has been a pattern of establishing links with other countries. When King George V died in 1936, the British Junior Red Cross was sent messages of sympathy by many other national societies and individual members in other countries.

During World War II, the Junior Red Cross was kept very busy. One group helped in a sick bay for evacuated children, in Shoreham-by-Sea in Sussex. The Detachment Commandant wrote: "Right well they worked, doing all that was asked of them, whether it was amusing and interesting, or dull and unpleasant." Other young members were given knitting patterns to make items for the troops. They received clear instructions: "articles in pairs – socks, gloves, cuffs, etc – should be fastened together, but do not sew them together; use a good sized safety pin - it, too, will come in very handy...".

In 1949, the Junior Red Cross was awarded royal recognition when Princess Elizabeth became its first Patron. When she succeeded to the throne in 1952, her young cousin, Princess Alexandra, then only 15 years old and still at school, took over the role. She was to take an active and lively interest in the Junior Red Cross for over 30 years. In 1983, the Princess of Wales agreed to become the latest royal patron.

Today, Youth and Junior groups are spread throughout the country. As the result of a review in 1993 entitled "Action with Humanity", the young people involved in Red Cross work have a clear and positive role both within the Society and in the community as a whole. This role is set not only to continue but to increase in importance into the next century through Red Cross Youth work with promoting international and cultural understanding, providing services to help people in crisis in local communities, and undertaking special projects such as helping on holidays for young people with disabilities and supporting people with HIV or AIDS.

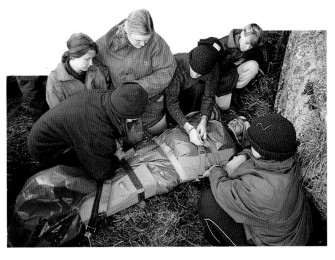

ACTION WITH HUMANITY

A major review of Red Cross Youth, seen here undertaking emergency rescue in 1994, has resulted in a modern focus.

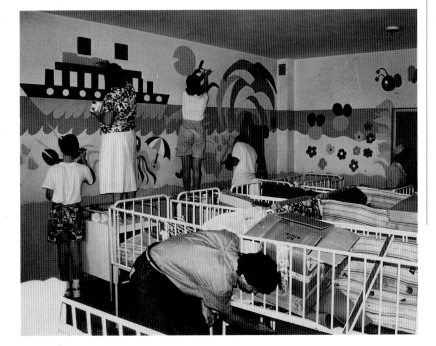

ORPHANAGE PAINTING

The winner of the "Create a Poster" competition in 1990 flew to Romania with two members of Red Cross Youth to see Red Cross work at first hand and to help paint this mural.

Tracing and Messages

DURING THE BATTLE OF SOLFERINO in 1859, Henry Dunant's concern was not solely to care physically for the wounded and dying, but also to ease the mental anguish of the soldiers, desperate to let their families know their fate.

"Oh Sir, if you could write to my father and ask him to comfort my mother" was a young corporal's typical request.

A SEARCHER'S ARMBAND

Searchers in World War II worked in hospitals throughout Great Britain and overseas in fighting zones.

Dunant organized a merchant volunteer to devote himself for two days to writing letters to the families of the dying. The Tracing and Message Service as it is today dates to the Franco-Prussian War of 1870–71, when an information and relief office for prisoners was established in Basle, Switzerland. The French and Prussian armies provided the relief office with lists of their prisoners so that families could obtain details of their loved ones.

Today, the needs of prisoners of war and missing persons, and of their families, are met by the Central Tracing Agency of the International Committee of the Red Cross. The International Welfare department of the British

THE FIRST SEARCH

The British Red Cross asked the army authorities for permission to search for wounded soldiers. Lord Kitchener's authorization marks the beginning of the Wounded and Missing Enquiry Bureau.

ENQUIRIES TO BRITAIN

This collection of letters is from national societies throughout the world investigating tracing enquiries.

Red Cross works with the International Red Cross and Red Crescent Movement. They are committed to establishing the whereabouts, health and welfare of relatives separated as a result of armed conflict, natural or other disasters, and to putting them in touch with each other.

The service has developed to provide information on civilian victims as well as prisoners of war. Some 25 per cent of the enquiries to the British Red Cross today are still from or concern victims of World War II.

More recent conflicts also have a great impact on this area of work. In 1993, for example, more than four million Red Cross messages between family members within

Bosnia and abroad in 99 different countries were exchanged at a rate of 100,000 per week. The Tracing and Message Service illustrates the unique capability of the Movement; those who undertake this work are a vital link in a worldwide humanitarian chain.

THE WOUNDED AND MISSING ENQUIRY BUREAU

Staff in the British Section in Geneva, Switzerland, pursued their painstaking work throughout World War I.

TOGETHER AT LAST

The dismantling of the Berlin Wall in 1989 led to a sharp increase in the number of tracing requests from families separated for almost 30 years.

COMMUNITY WORK

THROUGHOUT ITS HISTORY, the British Red Cross has undertaken humanitarian activities at home and abroad. Today, British Red Cross volunteers work in every local community providing services for people in crisis and in need of care. As an integral part of the International Red Cross and Red Crescent Movement, the largest voluntary humanitarian organization in the world, every member of the British Red Cross must abide by the fundamental principles of humanity, impartiality, neutrality, independence, voluntary service, unity and universality.

CARING FOR FRAIL PEOPLE

British Red Cross members are trained in the skills required to care for elderly people or people with disabilities, but they can also help with more everyday tasks that make life more enjoyable.

ON DUTY AT WHITE CITY

British Red Cross members provided first aid cover at White City football stadium in 1912.

It is the fundamental principles of the Red Cross Movement that enable the British Red Cross to do so much work in countries where it is too dangerous for other agencies to operate. And it is these same principles that dictate the work undertaken in every local community in Great Britain to care for people in crisis: the elderly, people with disabilities, the sick and the injured. Every day of the year, members of the British Red Cross provide essential services in local communities. They are part of a thriving organization with nearly 100,000 members working from branches and centres throughout the United Kingdom.

FIRST AID DUTY

One of the best-known and most visible of these everyday services is providing trained first aid cover at some 40,000 public events every year. Some of the events covered by the Society include the London to Brighton Bike Ride, the Great North Run, the Grand National and Badminton Horse Trials. The British Red Cross also has permanent nursing staff based at exhibition and events centres such as the Barbican Centre and Earls Court.

The Society has its own ambulance fleet, staffed by ambulance personnel who have received 100 hours of advanced training, much of which is delivered by professional ambulance trainers.

CARING FOR PEOPLE IN CRISIS

Throughout the country, British Red Cross members provide essential services for people with a range of different needs, aimed at making their lives fuller, more active or less isolated. The Transport and Escort service is provided for people who need to make essential journeys and who, for varying reasons, find it difficult to travel unaided or to use public transport. The service can help with short journeys such as getting to a medical appointment or doing the shopping. For long journeys, the British Red Cross operates a "network" system by which patients can be put on a train by members of one branch and met at the other end of the journey by representatives from another and driven to their destination.

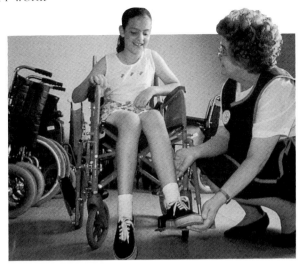

Another widely used service is Medical Loan. This provides equipment for short-term use by people in their homes – items such as backrests, bath seats, wheelchairs, commodes, walking sticks and frames are available from the 900 medical loan depots throughout the country. The service can sometimes allow a patient to leave hospital earlier than would otherwise have been possible, or enable someone to go on holiday who would be unable to transport their own equipment with them.

Returning home from a stay in hospital can be a difficult and worrying experience. The Home from Hospital scheme provides a co-ordinated system of hospital discharge and volunteer aftercare in collaboration with the statutory services. It ensures the smooth transition of patients from hospital to their own homes and supports them and their carers for up to four weeks afterwards.

After liaising with the health and social services professionals to assess the needs of the patient prior to discharge, a trained volunteer is then assigned to care for the patient on leaving hospital. This could include preparing the home for their return; providing personal care; preparing meals; providing respite for the client's carer; and accompanying the client on initial trips out of their home.

THERAPEUTIC BEAUTY CARE SERVICES

These include Hand Care, Therapeutic Beauty Care, Cosmetic Camouflage and Beauty Care Techniques for Blind

MEDICAL LOAN SERVICE

Providing essential medical equipment on short-term loan is a key service.

RED CROSS HOUSE, IRVINE

Red Cross House, in Scotland, assists people who have been inappropriately in long-stay hospitals or institutional care to establish themselves in the community. The complex provides services and accommodation for disabled people as well as day facilities.

People. The Hand and Beauty Care services are offered in such places as hospitals and residential homes, offering one-to-one contact and a chance for individuals to look and feel better. For people with conditions such as port wine stains or vitiligo, members trained in Cosmetic Camouflage can show them how to use specialized make-up to effectively camouflage areas of the skin and so avoid unwelcome stares from others. The Beauty Care Techniques for Blind People recognizes the importance of teaching women who cannot see how to apply make up by touch.

SPECIAL SERVICES, SPECIAL PEOPLE

Individual branches also organize services tailored to the specific needs of their areas; services such as residential homes for people with disabilities or innovative projects including a night watch scheme, a project to alleviate problems facing long-term carers, organizing holidays for children with disabilities or elderly, frail people or operating toy libraries. All these services rely on the network of volunteer members of the Society prepared to give their free time caring for others in crisis in their own communities. It is a tribute to each and every one that the services are provided with efficiency and skill, meeting real needs.

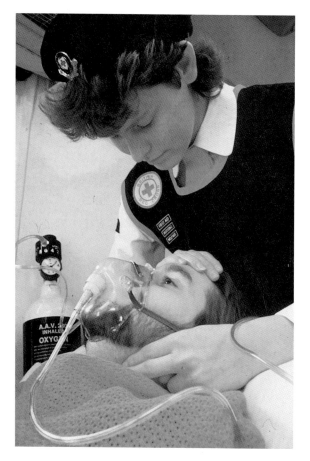

FIRST AID COVER

Trained British Red Cross members provide first aid cover at some 40,000 public events each year.

CARING IN THE HOME

Helping people in their own homes is a growing area of work for the Society, whether by providing short-term personal care or by offering to provide cover for someone's usual carer to enable them to have a break.

4

FINANCE AND PATRONAGE

This chapter describes the many and varied methods employed by the British Red Cross to raise funds, ranging from the first fundraising appeal of 1870, through the special funds, sales, and auctions of World War II, to the modern phenomena of direct mail, television appeals, and rock concerts. The tireless support of the Royal Family has been of vital importance to the British Red Cross since its foundation, as has the contribution made by the many famous personalities who give their time.

FUNDRAISING IN THE EARLY DAYS

FUNDRAISING HAS ALWAYS been key to the British Red Cross. Colonel Loyd-Lindsay (see pages 10-11) could be credited with being the first donor; he made an initial donation of £1,000. As a result of his initiative, contributions poured in. By the end of the Franco-Prussian War, almost £300,000 had been raised. In its early years, the fundraising efforts of the Society, solely in response to conflict, continued.

THE RED CROSS PEARLS

In 1918, Christie's held a special sale of donated pearls, many given in memory of loved ones. The pearls formed 41 necklaces and raised £84,383 19s 9d.

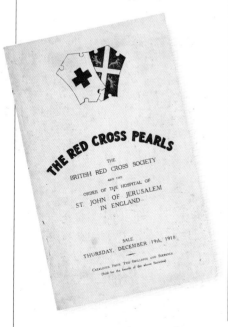

CHRISTIE'S SALESROOM

During World War I, Christie's held four general sales that raised £322,636 in funds for the British Red Cross.

1876–79

Between 1876 and 1879 the British Red Cross assisted in several conflicts including the Serbo-Turkish War, the Russo-Turkish War and the Zulu Wars. Over £40,000 was spent on medicine, hospital equipment and clothing during this three-year period.

1884–85

In February 1885, the Princess of Wales, later Queen Alexandra, formed a branch of the Red Cross. The Princess of Wales Branch raised £14,570 to deal with sick and wounded soldiers in Egypt and Sudan. The National Society spent an additional £19,352.

THE MOST URGENT FUND

Poster artist Tom Purvis designed this poster at the start of his career. It was one of a number specially commissioned by the Joint War Committee from prominent artists.

LITTLE NANCY

Three-year-old Nancy used her toy ambulance to collect donations for the Mayor of Camberwell's Red Cross Fund and to distribute free cigarettes to soldiers in local hospitals.

1897

In 1897 Turkey and Greece went to war. Some £3,100 was spent in Greece and £2,500 in Turkey. Much of the money was spent on clothing and food distribution for refugees rather than on wounded soldiers who were felt to be less in need.

1899–1902

With the threat of the second Boer War looming, the Central British Red Cross Committee met to agree on the division of work between the various societies. The British Red Cross was made responsible, among other tasks, for "all subscriptions from the public on behalf of the sick and wounded". In October 1899, Lord Wantage wrote to *The Times* appealing for funds. In total, some £500,000 was raised, including £9,000 donated by the Princess of Wales, the balance of the fund collected in her name in 1885.

1914–18

When World War I broke out in 1914, Queen Alexandra made an appeal in the press for funds: "Much money will be needed and many gifts if we are faithfully to discharge our trust and be able to say, when all is over, that we have done all we could for the comfort and relief of our sick and wounded."

On 2 October, the Society appealed in *The Times* for funds to provide motor ambulances. One vehicle cost £400 and, as a result of the appeal, enough money to buy 512 ambulances was raised within three weeks. By the end of the war the stores department, which was responsible for distributing all the equipment to hospitals, had distributed goods to the value of £1,480,217. The British Red Cross Society had raised £21,885,035 and spent £20,058,355 on hospitals, medicine, clothing, grants and aftercare to the sick and wounded.

POSTAGE LABELS

The first postage label (bottom left) was issued during the Balkan War. The others here date from World War I; the top two were from a set of six costing 6d that sold in their hundreds of thousands.

FUNDRAISING IN WORLD WAR II

THE DUKE OF GLOUCESTER'S Red Cross and St John Appeal was launched in September 1939 and became the largest charitable fund of its day. Thousands of volunteers arranged fundraising events, organized house-to-house collections and packed prisoner of war parcels. The fundraising was so successful that by 1946 it had raised over £54 million, a staggering amount for the time.

THE INAUGURATION OF THE PENNY-A-WEEK FUND

The Penny-a-Week Fund, begun in 1940, and the Rural Pennies scheme were hugely successful.

AID TO RUSSIA FUND

This, the only separate fund in World War II, was personally led by Mrs Clementine Churchill and raised £7.25 million.

One of the most successful appeals was the Penny-a-Week Fund. The fundraising was based on collecting a penny a week from workers as well as organizing house-to-house collections. In 1940, £100,000 was raised in only eight weeks. By the end of the war the employees of 70,000 firms and organizations were contributing to the scheme, raising over £17 million, more than a third of the whole sum raised by the appeal.

FLAG DAYS

These played an important part in wartime fundraising. During June, July and August 1940, over £578,000 was raised. When the collecting boxes were opened, many people had donated their wedding rings.

The slogan for the flag day in 1941 was provided by a young girl who worked in a Red Cross office in London. One night, when she was on duty as a fire-watcher, her suburb was badly bombed. The following morning, when she arrived at her office, she declared, "Anyone who has seen the Red Cross work in a blitz will certainly give a little extra this year."

ON THE RIGHT TRACK

This promotional poster, based on a famous Southern Railways poster, was produced specially to encourage employees to donate to the Penny-a-Week Fund.

STREET COLLECTIONS

VADs, seen here outside Hammersmith Detachment Headquarters, joined the tremendous fundraising effort.

AGRICULTURAL FUNDS, SALES AND AUCTIONS

The war, of course, did not just affect those living in towns and cities. The Red Cross Agriculture Fund was formed to secure the help of those working in the countryside and by 1945 there were 18,000 committees throughout Britain. The Fund supported a variety of different initiatives including sales of flowers, farm produce and livestock. The Milk Marketing Board persuaded over 15,000 milk producers to donate 2s 6d per quarter from their milk cheques, raising £10,000 a year. Twenty thousand children were recruited to onion-growing clubs, providing extra onions for the services while the Fund received the revenue from the sales. By 1946 the Fund had raised over £8 million.

Many sales and auctions were held during the war; the first at Christies in 1940, which included a diamond and sapphire brooch donated by Queen Mary, an anonymously donated Rolls Royce, and a sampler worked by Charlotte Brontë at the age of 12, raised £120,000. Other sales held at Christies included ones for stamps, wine, cigars and contemporary paintings. Debenhams department store held a jewellery sale, Sotheby's auctioneers held a book sale and Claridges hotel organized an exhibition and sale of lace. Other appeals were made from the worlds of sport, entertainment, education, religion and the media.

FUNDRAISING TODAY

FUNDRAISING FOR THE British Red Cross today is a varied and long-term occupation. It includes high-profile appeals and events as well as behind-the-scenes fundraising methods such as direct mail, flag days and shops. However the money is raised, the British Red Cross must spend it wisely.

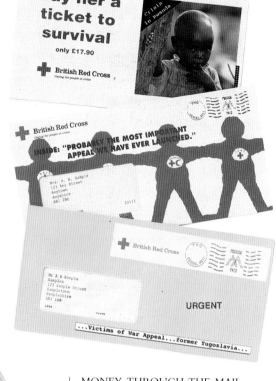

THE 125 SOCIETY

Launched in November 1994, the 125 Society is a means of ensuring regular income – every member signs up to donate at least £1,000 per year – and of encouraging influential people to support the work of the Society. Members of the 125 Society are entitled to wear the pin shown above.

MONEY THROUGH THE MAIL

When the Society must compete for financial support, fundraising materials need to be innovative and compelling.

Although major events have an important part to play, not only in raising money but also in increasing public awareness, other, less high-profile, fundraising methods are vital to the continuing ability of the British Red Cross to provide its essential services.

The support of companies, large and small, is imperative. British Red Cross policy is to develop long-lasting relationships with the private business sector. Whether support is given by donating money, donating gifts in kind or by encouraging employees to support the Society, its potential is enormous. As part of this policy, the British Red Cross has a panel of business leaders who actively promote the interests of the Society within the corporate world as well as giving their invaluable expert advice and support.

DIRECT MARKETING

One of the most successful "behind-the-scenes" fundraising methods used by the Society is direct marketing. By developing fundraising links with both individual donors and businesses, direct marketing creates a constantly expanding base of people sympathetic to the

Red Cross Shop

FUNDRAISING ON THE HIGH STREET

The British Red Cross has over 300 shops around the country, all selling a range of good quality, second-hand goods, including clothes, books and bric-a-brac. They provide a steady source of income for the Society and are a constant reminder of the need for funds.

work of the Society; it can call on these people in times of emergency as well as to support day-to-day activities. Another crucial area of fundraising is to encourage supporters either to remember the Society in their wills or to covenant their donations over four years, so providing a stable source of income. Without this, planning the future work of the British Red Cross would be impossible.

RED CROSS WEEK

Always held around World Red Cross Day on 8 May, the birthday of the Movement's founder, Henry Dunant, Red Cross Week is an annual nationwide fundraising week during which members in every branch organize house-to-house collections and fundraising events. There have been many varied and unusual events planned by individual branches, from sponsored mountain climbing and plastic duck races to highland flings!

In 1994, the message "We're pinning our hopes on you" was adopted and a distinctive Red Cross lapel pin was given in return for a donation. Its marked success, both in increasing funds raised and in raising awareness of Red Cross Week, has ensured that this campaign will continue in the coming years.

THE LIFEBLOOD OF THE SOCIETY

However funds are raised, and for whichever aspect of its work, money is vital to the Society. The British Red Cross does not receive grants from government departments except for specifically approved projects such as international disaster relief and development projects overseas. So the support of individuals and companies who embrace the work and the ideals of the Society is crucial if its work in caring for people in crisis both at home and overseas is to continue.

THE RED CROSS PIN

This lapel pin, given to those who donate during Red Cross Week, was developed in 1994 to encourage larger donations and to raise awareness of the week.

Major Fundraising Campaigns

SOME CONFLICTS AND NATURAL DISASTERS of the 1990s, such as the plight of the Kurds in Iraq, the tragedies of Somalia, former Yugoslavia and Rwanda, capture the public's attention and necessitate major fundraising campaigns. Money raised cannot be used for any other projects, local community work or general administration costs.

POT OF GOLD AUCTION

The auctioneering talents of Jeffrey Archer and Robert Kilroy-Silk raised £150,000 for the people of Somalia. The appeal total was £1.3 million.

SIMPLE TRUTH CAMPAIGN

In April 1991, the plight of Kurdish refugees fleeing Iraq into Turkey and Iran was witnessed by millions on television. Author Jeffrey Archer, together with John Gray, Director of Public Affairs at the British Red Cross, and his team, launched a campaign called The Simple Truth after a song released in aid of the appeal by Chris de Burgh. A rock concert at Wembley Arena was organized in just three weeks.

SOMALIA APPEAL

Shortly after the British Red Cross launched an appeal to provide aid for the people of war- and famine-ravaged Somalia in 1992, an 82-year-old widow, with no money to give, donated her wedding ring instead. This simple act led to a

APPEAL FOR SOMALIA LOGO

The map of Africa made from a gold necklace caught the public's imagination and ensured success.

LOTS FOR THE POT OF GOLD

Items to be auctioned for Somalia were previewed by BBC's The Clothes Show. They included a Fabergé brooch once owned by the last Tsarina of Russia and a specially designed Somalia jewel depicting an ear of wheat and a teardrop.

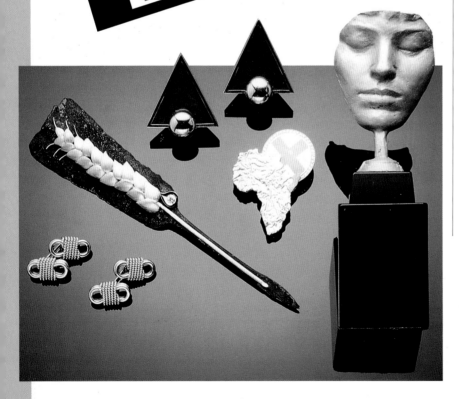

campaign chaired by volunteer Jonathan Stone asking people to donate jewellery to be sold at a Phillips auction at the Savoy Hotel on 14 February 1993. The public, celebrities and the Royal Family responded with amazing generosity.

FORMER YUGOSLAVIA APPEAL

The continuing and increasing hardship facing the civilians of former Yugoslavia led to the launch of the Victims of War Appeal. Based on the slogan "£10 buys a Red Cross food parcel that will feed a family of four for a month", the appeal was launched in the summer of 1993 by presenter Nick Ross and raised some £5,000,000.

The appeal was supported by a gala evening at the English National Opera, attended by The Princess of Wales. The BBC's "Challenge Anneka" team helped by refurbishing a school that had been destroyed by mortar attack.

SIMPLE TRUTH CONCERT

M C Hammer (above) and Chris de Burgh (left) were just two of the many stars who performed at The Simple Truth concert. The concert was televised live and networked to 24 countries. An appeal for credit card donations was made during the concert, which raised £13,832,000 in the UK alone.

ROYAL PATRONAGE IN THE EARLY DAYS

THE BRITISH ROYAL FAMILY has a long history of involvement with the British Red Cross. At its foundation in 1870, Queen Victoria became Patron of the Society and the Prince of Wales, later King Edward VII, its President. Queen Victoria took a deep and sympathetic interest in the work of the Society, describing it after the Serbo-Turkish War of 1876 as "indeed the work of a Good Samaritan…".

1844-1925 QUEEN ALEXANDRA

This commemorative postcard (right), produced during World War I, clearly expresses the high esteem in which Queen Alexandra was held.

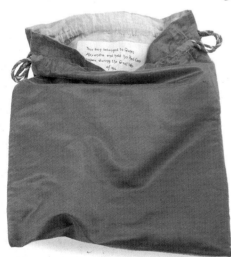

1914-8 QUEEN ALEXANDRA'S RED CROSS BAG

Throughout World War I, Queen Alexandra carried her Red Cross papers in this bag.

In February 1885, the Princess of Wales, later Queen Alexandra, formed a branch whose purpose was to raise funds to send medical and other luxuries to sick and wounded British soldiers and sailors in Egypt and Sudan, and to provide the troops with amusements, games, books and small comforts. In a letter written in August 1885, Brigadier-General J. Hudson, commanding at Suakim, expressed his heartfelt thanks: "It is impossible to value too highly the assistance we have received from the Princess of Wales' Branch… in the generous gifts, it has [provided] almost every conceivable comfort and luxury to our hospitals and the men in camps. In no previous campaign have I ever seen anything like it…"

THE ROYAL CHARTER

In 1908, Queen Alexandra, by then President of the Society, signed the petition for the granting of a Royal Charter. This was approved by the Privy Council and the Charter was granted on 3 September 1908. When World War I broke out in 1914, Queen Alexandra appealed to the public: "Thousands of our brave sailors and soldiers are standing ready to defend Britain's shores and to uphold her honour. Their sufferings will be great, and it is to us that they will look for comfort and relief. As President of the British Red Cross Society, I appeal for all your help. I do it knowing that you will respond to this appeal in the name of humanity." Queen Alexandra's death in 1925 deprived the Society of a president who had been unflagging in her support and encouragement for over a quarter of a century.

KING GEORGE AND QUEEN ELIZABETH

In 1936, the new King George VI granted his patronage to the Society while his wife, Queen Elizabeth, assumed the office of President. As Duke of York, the King had been closely involved with the work of the Society as Chairman of Council. Throughout the following years, and most particularly during the dark days of World War II, the support and encouragement of the King and Queen proved inestimable. With the outbreak of war in 1939, the Society formed committees to raise vital funds. One such was the Agriculture Fund and there is a lasting memorial to it in Windsor Great Park. When the fund reached £5 million, five red oaks were planted in Windsor Great Park by members of the Royal Family. When the fund closed in 1945, the King commanded that a further four oaks should be planted to form the shape of a cross. A plaque at the site bears the following inscription selected by King George:

"Through God's great grace, through strength of English oak, We have preserved our faith, our Throne, our land; Now, with our freedom saved from tyrant's yoke, We plant these trees. Remember why they stand."

In 1947, after the end of the war, Queen Elizabeth officially opened Barnett Hill in Wonersh, Surrey, as the Red Cross training centre. The house, a wartime convalescent home, was donated to the Society by its owner, Mrs Cook. On presenting the keys, she said: "For those who in future come here to be trained in the work of the Red Cross there will be the inspiration of the knowledge that they follow the example of devotion and duty given to them by their beloved Queen." Barnett Hill is still the British Red Cross Society's national training centre.

1918 PRINCESS MARY

Like her mother, Princess Mary was an active supporter of the British Red Cross, becoming the first Commandant-in-Chief of the Voluntary Aid Detachments (see pages 28–29) in 1926.

1953 PRINCESS MARY'S TROPICAL CAP

Between 1953 and 1960 Princess Mary, the Princess Royal, visited several British Red Cross branches in the Caribbean and in Nigeria.

1940 KING GEORGE AND QUEEN ELIZABETH

King George and Queen Elizabeth visiting the motor convoy leaving for France during World War II.

ROYAL PATRONAGE TODAY

TODAY'S ROYAL FAMILY are no less generous with their time and support than their predecessors. At some point over the past ten years, almost every member of the family has attended a British Red Cross event, bringing vital publicity and awareness to the Society's work. Several hold positions within the Society: Queen Elizabeth, Queen Elizabeth The Queen Mother, The Princess of Wales and Princess Alexandra.

QUEEN ELIZABETH
THE QUEEN MOTHER

The Queen Mother opens the reception at national headquarters in London, 1992.

QUEEN ELIZABETH

Her Majesty The Queen, Patron and President of the Society, presents Dr Ahmed Hassan of the Somali Red Crescent with the Movement's Prize for Peace and Humanity, in recognition of that Society's outstanding work during the civil war and famine in 1992.

HER MAJESTY THE QUEEN, PATRON AND PRESIDENT

Her Majesty The Queen was the first Royal Patron of Red Cross Youth, a position she relinquished when she became the Society's Patron and President on her accession to the throne. She is regularly updated on the work of the Society and has taken the opportunity to see members at work both at national headquarters and in visits to branches.

In October 1993, Her Majesty gave the keynote speech at the Council of Delegates, the body that brings together the International Committee of the Red Cross, the International Federation and national societies. She praised the work of the Movement and called on others to ensure that that work can continue: "The sanctity of your emblems and the freedom for those engaged in your work to do so without challenge or fear must be respected."

HER MAJESTY QUEEN ELIZABETH THE QUEEN MOTHER, DEPUTY PRESIDENT

Her Majesty Queen Elizabeth The Queen Mother, Deputy President since 1953, has the longest association of the Royal family with the Society. As President during World War II, she gave unfailing support in encouraging members in the massive programme of work and the appeals for vital funds.

Her Majesty continues to show her support for the work of the Society. During the Pot of Gold Appeal for Somalia (see pages 80–81), Her Majesty generously donated an ornate writing desk which alone raised £10,000.

Her Royal Highness Princess Alexandra was the longest-serving Patron of Red Cross Youth, holding the position from 1953 to 1983. During that time she took a tremendous interest in the work of the young members of the Society.

HER ROYAL HIGHNESS PRINCESS ALEXANDRA

An active and much-admired supporter of the British Red Cross since she became Patron of Red Cross Youth in 1953, a position she held for 30 years, Princess Alexandra showed a keen interest in and dedication to the Youth and Juniors throughout.

A Vice President of the British Red Cross since 1981, Princess Alexandra undertakes a wide range of engagements with the Society each year, visiting projects throughout the country and lending her vital support to national fundraising events.

HER ROYAL HIGHNESS THE PRINCESS OF WALES

Since becoming Patron of Red Cross Youth in 1983, a position she still holds, the Princess of Wales has had an increasing role with the Society. In 1993 she became a Vice President, in 1994 a member of the Advisory Commission on the future of the Movement and in 1995 Patron of the Society's 125th Birthday Appeal.

The Princess of Wales takes particular interest in the Society's work overseas, visiting projects in, among others, Nepal and Zimbabwe. Her Royal Highness is also a keen supporter of the essential fund- and awareness-raising campaigns, attending events such as The Simple Truth concert for Kurdish refugees, fundraising lunches with the business world, and the Membership Gala at the Royal Albert Hall to present the first Care in Crisis Awards.

THE PRINCESS OF WALES

Patron of Red Cross Youth, Her Royal Highness distributes food at a feeding programme during a four-day visit to Zimbabwe in 1993.

Famous Personalities

PUBLICITY IS VITAL TO the British Red Cross, whether to raise awareness of its work, to attract more supporters, to highlight a particular event or, most importantly, to help raise funds. The support of well-known personalities is essential. By lending their names to a particular cause, these individuals can help to generate much-needed media coverage and encourage their own supporters to help.

WALT DISNEY AT THE EUROPEAN PREMIERE OF *PETER PAN*

An ambulance driver for the American Red Cross during World War I, Walt Disney donated the profits from the 1953 première to the British Red Cross.

The British Red Cross has always actively encouraged the support of well-known personalities who have had a marked impact on public awareness of a given cause. Some have contributed money directly, like Walt Disney, who donated the proceeds of the première of *Peter Pan* in London, and Sinead O'Connor, who donated her home in Los Angeles to the Pot of Gold Appeal for Somalia. Others, like Nigel Havers, have travelled overseas to see for themselves the work of the Red Cross and so attracted all-important publicity to that work. Others still have themselves benefited from British Red Cross services.

NIGEL HAVERS IN CROATIA

The actor Nigel Havers has twice travelled to former Yugoslavia, in 1993 and 1994, bringing vital publicity to the need for funds.

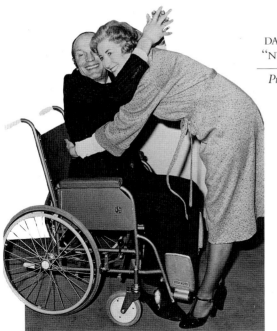

HENRY COOPER AND DAME VERA LYNN LAUNCH "NURSING FOR THE FAMILY"

Publicity for new initiatives, as here in 1976, is essential in order to inform the public that the British Red Cross can help.

More conventionally, others give their time to work on committees or to act as the spearhead of an appeal; for example Angela Rippon is Chair of the 125 Society.

However they show their support, there can be no doubt that each and every "celebrity" who has helped the British Red Cross has made a marked difference to its fund- and awareness-raising efforts, and so has ensured that the Society is better able to care for people in crisis both at home and overseas.

After falling and twisting her ankle while starring in the play *Little Foxes*, Elizabeth Taylor borrowed a wheelchair from the Kensington and Chelsea Medical Loan depot, appearing in it on stage. She later autographed the back of the chair so that it could be auctioned.

SUPPORT FROM SIMON WESTON

Himself a victim of conflict, Simon Weston was so moved by the plight of civilians in former Yugoslavia that he launched his own appeal in 1992.

A GALAXY OF STARS PUBLICIZE THE POT OF GOLD APPEAL FOR SOMALIA

From left to right, Gloria Hunniford, Felicity Kendal, Jeffrey Archer, Peter Bowles, Rula Lenska, Peter Egan and Nerys Hughes cut into a cake made by Jane Asher in 1992.

WHERE YOUR MONEY GOES

THE BRITISH RED CROSS is self-financing and receives no grants from government departments except for specifically approved projects. The main sources of funds are appeal donations, legacies, investment income, corporate and individual donors and national fundraising activities.

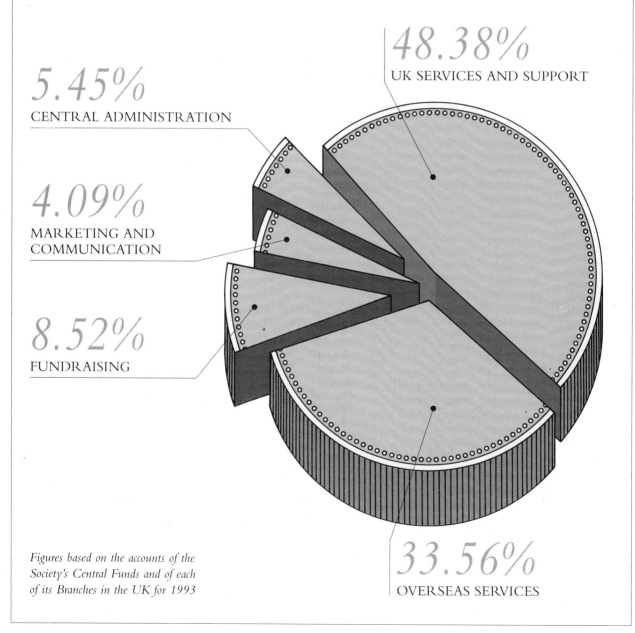

48.38%
UK SERVICES AND SUPPORT

5.45%
CENTRAL ADMINISTRATION

4.09%
MARKETING AND COMMUNICATION

8.52%
FUNDRAISING

33.56%
OVERSEAS SERVICES

Figures based on the accounts of the Society's Central Funds and of each of its Branches in the UK for 1993

FUTURE
OF THE
SOCIETY

The Director General of the British Red Cross, Mike Whitlam, examines the current and future role of the Society. He describes the importance of prioritizing resources and the response of the International Federation of Red Cross and Red Crescent Societies to the increasing numbers of vulnerable people worldwide. Mike Whitlam also explores the developing capability of the Society to provide emergency and community relief and stresses the importance of recruiting and training volunteers. Finally, he sets out the British Red Cross's increasingly important contribution to developing policy within the International Movement.

THE AIMS OF THE BRITISH RED CROSS

THE PAST 125 YEARS have seen the British Red Cross develop and grow. Throughout its history, the Society has responded to changing needs caused by changing circumstances. Through war, peace, natural and unnatural disaster, its members have striven to provide effective, humanitarian and practical help to those in need. That it has done so effectively is a tribute to all those who have given their time to care impartially for others and who continue to provide ever more relevant services.

It is this impartiality that has given the whole Red Cross and Red Crescent Movement a unique role in so many disaster situations: often, the Movement can carry out its vital work in areas where no other agency can operate. The protection the Geneva Conventions accord to those working under the sign of the red cross or red crescent has saved literally millions of lives; not just those of the personnel involved in relief missions, but also the lives of those in desperate need of aid.

SKILLS AND KNOWLEDGE

Experience of some of the more difficult and dangerous situations has helped to provide the skills and knowledge that make the work of the British Red Cross in this country both effective and relevant. Skills in modern first aid techniques, listening, lifting and handling, ambulance aid, rescue, logistics and many others, ensure that the British Red Cross is ready to respond to almost any modern crisis.

EMERGENCY SERVICE

The British Red Cross is actively developing its capacity to assist the emergency services at times of disaster in peacetime.

PRIORITIZING RESOURCES

Today, the British Red Cross is operating in an environment of shrinking monetary resources and increasing numbers of people in need. There is a real necessity, therefore, for the Society to prioritize its resources effectively so that it is reaching those who are most in need, both at home and overseas.

People's lives can change suddenly and dramatically, leaving them feeling helpless and vulnerable. Most recently, the peoples of former Yugoslavia and of Rwanda have been shattered by the terrible wars in their countries; the floods in Wales changed people's lives in hours; the earthquakes in India, Japan, Turkey and the United States left people homeless and desperate for food and shelter. These crises were of such a scale that the impact put the Red Cross and Red Crescent Movement in the public eye. Yet there are other, smaller crises that have an equal impact on individuals.

A WORKPLAN FOR THE VULNERABLE

The worldwide recession has led to a marked reduction in economic aid to the poorest nations. Here in the United Kingdom, the economic recession is continuing and there are high levels of unemployment. In these circumstances, charities such as the British Red Cross are finding it increasingly difficult to raise the necessary income. At the same time, the number of those affected by crises is increasing in line with the number of people made vulnerable through poverty. The worldwide population below the poverty line exceeds one billion. These people are vulnerable because their poverty forces them to live close to hazards, on flood plains for example; they are vulnerable because they are subjected to violence or discrimination; they are vulnerable because the traditional welfare net provided by governments is being eroded in almost every country.

The International Federation of Red Cross and Red Crescent Societies has responded to this situation by developing a strategic workplan with national societies to ensure that they are capable of responding to the needs of the most vulnerable. For this, "vulnerable" has been defined as "those at greatest risk from situations that threaten their survival or their capacity to live with a minimum of social and economic security and human dignity".

In order to achieve its objectives in the future, the British Red Cross is undertaking a major research project in Great Britain to establish which are the most vulnerable groups. The results of this research will influence the programmes it undertakes into the next century. Work is also underway to ensure that British Red Cross branches throughout the country are providing the most relevant

CARING FOR THE VULNERABLE

Today, many thousands of people are made vulnerable because they are subjected to violence or discrimination. Here, Director General of the British Red Cross Mike Whitlam visits a Red Cross centre in Somalia.

PROVIDING ECONOMIC AID

The worldwide recession has resulted in less economic aid to the poorest nations.

INTERNATIONAL INFLUENCE

The British Red Cross plays a key role in discussing and developing policy and practice within the Movement.

GRANDE-BRETAGNE

services to the vulnerable groups in their area, and that these services are offered to the highest possible standard. Given the very real need to prioritize available resources, all current services are being reviewed to ensure that the most relevant are developed and strengthened.

EMERGENCY SERVICES

The emergency services provided by the British Red Cross are paramount; emergencies can have a devastating effect on the most vulnerable. The Society, therefore, is actively developing its capacity to assist the emergency services in peacetime as well as the military medical authorities in times of war. The branches are working to develop and strengthen their emergency response capacity and are encouraging regular training exercises to ensure that their plans are effective. The services provided to the community have an emergency bias. The most recent example is the newly developed Fire Victim Support Scheme (see pages 42-43).

RECRUITMENT OF VOLUNTEERS

"Resources" does not refer solely to income; trained volunteers are vital if services are to be delivered. A major priority, therefore, for the near future is the recruitment of committed volunteers who are willing to offer their time to help others within their own communities. An active recruitment and support programme is underway. As well as using television and press to recruit new volunteers, new support packs and contracts have been developed.

DISASTER REPONSE

Internationally, the British Red Cross is working to improve further its disaster response. The Society has taken a leading role in the development of a pan-European logistics network. Once in place, this will help to co-ordinate a central European warehouse for rapid disaster response. The British Red Cross plays an important role in the international aid world and aims to develop the thinking and practice that help to make the response to disasters worldwide more effective. The skills and qualities of British Red Cross delegates (see pages 56–57) are known throughout the world.

OVERSEAS AID

The British Red Cross is also increasing its overseas aid activities. The number of skilled delegates working overseas increases year by year (172 in 1993); work is underway to improve the British Red Cross's ability to assess disaster situations quickly and to co-ordinate its activities to provide sudden disaster assistance in both the short and medium term. The Society is also working with other national societies on a portfolio of sustainable development projects that will ensure a better readiness on the part of those national societies to respond when major disasters do occur.

For the British Red Cross, the end of this century will be a time of consolidation and planning. It will be a time of change, responding to the changing environment. It will also be a time of growth: growth in knowledge and understanding; growth in capability to respond to need; growth in those services caring for the most vulnerable. One of the real strengths of the Society over the past 125 years has been its ability to recognize changing needs and to develop its response effectively. This decade has been another vital stage in that development; the result will be a stronger Society really capable of helping those who are most vulnerable in our communities, both at home and overseas.

WORKING INTERNATIONALLY

One of 163 national societies around the world, the British Red Cross plays a key role within the International Movement. The Society is a representative on the Executive Council of the Federation; its Chairman of Council, the Countess of Limerick, was elected a Vice President of the Federation in 1993; and its Vice President, the Princess of Wales, is a member of the Advisory Commission on the future of the Red Cross and Red Crescent Movement. Through the Director General, the Society is also a member of the European Community Liaison Bureau. The Director General is also Chairman of the Co-ordinating Group of Donor Societies (G24).

At International Red Cross and Red Crescent meetings over the past few years, British Red Cross experts have addressed diverse but important subjects pertinent to the Movement as a whole. These include the important areas of fundraising, the effective procurement and delivery of aid, aspects of conflict such as the indiscriminate deployment of mines and the use of food and water supplies as weapons of war. Other subjects have included global issues such as preventative diplomacy and the release of hostages.

It is vital that the British Red Cross continues to share its knowledge and expertise and that it maintains an active role in discussing and developing policy and practice internationally.

EFFECTIVE DISASTER RESPONSE

The British Red Cross has taken a leading part in working to ensure that the international response to disasters is as effective as possible.

INDEX

Page numbers in italic refer to
illustrations and captions

A

Aberfan, *46*
Afghanistan, *59*
Agricultural Fund, 77, 83
aims, 15, 90-4
air ambulance, 43, *43*
air raids, 32-3
   training, 62-3, *62*
Alexandra, Princess, 67, 85, *85*
Alexandra, Queen (Princess of Wales), 13,
   15, 74, 75, 82, *82*
ambulances, 42-3, 75
appeals *see* fundraising
Archer, Elizabeth, *57*
Archer, Jeffrey, 80, 80, 87
Army Medical Service, 15
Asher, Jane, 87
Australia, flood relief, 41
Austrian Gold Medal, *44*
awards, 16-17

B

Balkan conflicts, 13, 25, 29
Balkan War Medal, *16*, 17
Barnett Hill, 83
Bertschinger, Claire, 16
blood transfusion service, 30-1
Boer Wars, 12, 24, 25, 75
Bowles, Peter, *87*
branches, 19
British Honduras, 46-7, *46*
Brittain, Vera, *28*
Bulgaria, 66

C

Cambodia, 52, *59*
Cantlie, Sir James, 64, *65*
Care in Crisis Award, *17*
Central Council Branch, 19
Central Red Cross Committee, 15
Changi quilt, *38*, 39
Channel Islands, 36-7
children's nurseries, *36*
Christian of Schleswig Holstein, Princess,
   10, *11*
Christie, Agatha, *28*
Churchill, Clementine, 76
community work, 61-72
   first-aid posts, 70
   training, 62-3
convalescence, *37*
Cooper, Henry, *87*
Council, 18
Cowan, Major, 42
Crewe, Jessie, *29*

D

Davidson, Henry, 8
de Burgh, Chris, 80, *81*
Deakin, Jenny, *57*
Dennys, Joyce, *15*
Diana, Princess of Wales, 67, 81, 85, *85*
direct marketing, fundraising, 78-9
disaster response time, 60
Disasters Emergency Committee (DEC),
   47
Disney, Walt, 86, *86*
displaced persons, 37
Duke of Gloucester's Appeal, 76
Dunant, Henry, 6, 67, 68, 79

E

Edward VII, King, 10, 13, 82
Egan, Peter, 87
Egyptian campaign, 24, 74, 82
Elizabeth, Queen Mother, 83, 84, *84*
Elizabeth II, Queen, 67, 84, *84*
emblem, 6, 9
emergency relief, 41-60, *90*
   personnel, 56-7
   response times, 60
   sphere of operations, 58-9
   transporting supplies, 50-1
   transporting victims, 42-3
emergency services, 92
Empey, Dr, 31
establishment, 8-9
Ethiopia, 31, *31*, *51*, 52-3
European First Aid Competition, *63*
evacuation, 36

F

finance, expenditure, 88
   fundraising, 74-81
Fire Victim Support Unit, *42*, 43, 55
first aid posts, 70
fishing fleets, 30, *31*
flag days, 77
flood relief, 41
Florence Nightingale Medal, *16*, 17
food parcels, 34-5
foundation, 6-21
Franco-Prussian War, 10, 12, 13, 50, 74
fundraising, 74-81
   early days, 11, 74-5
   famous personalities, 86-7
   major campaigns, 80-1
   modern, 78-9
   World War II, 76-7
Furley, Sir John, 12, *12*
Furse, Dame Katherine, 27

G

gas decontamination, *63*
Geneva Conventions, 6, 7, 9, 90
George VI, King, 83
Gibbs, Sir Philip, 66
Gold Coast Branch, *20*

[Continuation]

Goodwin, Sir John, 26
Gray, John, 80
Greece, 25
Gulf War, 54

H

Hammer, M C, *81*
Hampstead floods, 48
Hassan, Ahmed, *84*
Havers, Nigel, 86, *86*
headquarters, 18
Herald of Free Enterprise, 52
Home from Hospital scheme, 70
Hong Kong, *21*
hop-picking, 30, *31*
horse-drawn ambulances, *42*
hospital ships, *42*
hospital trains, 25, *25*, *42*, 43
Hudson, J, 82
Hughes, Nerys, 87
Hungarian refugees, 40, *44*, 45, *45*
Hunniford, Gloria, 87
Hurricane Hattie, 46-7, *46*

I

India, cyclones, 49
Indo-Pakistan border conflict, 41
International Commitee, 7, 8
International Federation of Red Cross and
   Red Crescent Societies, 9
International Tracing and Message
   Service, 58
Iran, 47, *47*
Iraq, 54, *54*, 80
Islamic world, 9

J

Joint War Committee, 26
Joint War Organization, 32
Junior Red Cross, 66-7

K

Kendall, Felicity, 87
Keogh, Alfred, 26
Kilroy-Silk, Robert, 80
Korean War, 44
Kurds, 54, 80

L

Lack, Steven, 17
League of Red Cross and Red Crescent
   Societies, 9, 13
Lenska, Rula, 86
Limerick, Angela, Countess of, 14, *14*
Limerick, Sylvia, Countess of, 14, *14*
local communities, 70-1
Lockerbie, 52
Loyd-Lindsay, Colonel, 10, *11*, 74

Loyd-Lindsay, Mrs, *11*
Lynn, Dame Vera, 87
Lynton and Lynmouth floods, 44-5, *45*

M

McIntosh, John, 13, *13*
Malawi, *20*
manuals, 64-5
Mary, Princess Royal, *83*
Mary, Princess of Teck, *11*
Mary, Queen, 77
Masefield, John, *28*
medals, 16-17
Medical Loan Service, 70, *70*
Melley, John, 31, *31*
membership, 19
Merrick, John, 12
Meyrick, Francis, 56
Michael, Jonathan, *56*
Milk Marketing Board, 77
Ministry of Defence, 18
Monkhouse, Muriel, 14
Morocco, 46
Muriel Monkhouse Award, 17

N

national societies, 22
National Society for the Aid to the Sick
    and Wounded in War, 12
National Youth Forum, 18
Netley, 26, *27*
neutrality, 6
New Forest fire, 48
Nightingale, Florence, 10, *11*, 25
Norwich City football violence, 48, *49*

O

objectives, 8, 15
O'Connor, Sinead, 86
Oliver, Percy Lane, 30-1
Order of St John, 26, 32
origins, 6-7
overseas aid, 92-3
overseas branches, 20-1
Overseas Central Council Branch, 19

P

Palestinian refugees, 40
patronage, early days, 82-3
    today, 84-5
Penny-a-Week Fund, *76*, 77
Piper Alpha, 53
Plummer, Arnold, *56*
postage labels, 75
Pot of Gold Appeal, *80*, 86, 87
Princess Christian hospital trains, 25, *25*
Princess of Wales Branch, 74
principles, 8, 15
prisoners of war, 34-5, *37*
    creativity, 38-9
    tracing service, 68-9

Protocols, 9
publications, 64-5
Purvis, Tom, *75*

Q

quilts, 38-9

R

recruitment, 92
Red Crescent, emblem, 6, 9, 24
Red Cross Clinic for Rheumatic Diseases,
    13
Red Cross parcels, 27, 34-5
Red Cross House, *70*
Red Cross Week, 79
Red Cross Youth, 66-7
Reekie, Miss, *41*
relief parcels, 27, 34-5
relief work, 40-1
Rhodesian Branch, *21*
Rippon, Angela, 87
Ross, Nick, 81
Royal Charter of Incorporation, 15, 82
royal patronage, 82-5
    early days, 82-3
    today, 84-5
Russo-Turkish war, 24, 56-7, 74
Rwanda, *54*, 55, *59*

S

St Andrew's Ambulance Association, 64
St John Ambulance Association, 12, 64
Serbo-Bulgarian war, 24, 25
Serbo-Turkish war, 24
Sewell, Annie, *56*
ships, *42*, *50*
Simple Truth Campaign, 80, *81*, *85*
Singapore, 38-9
Solferino, Battle of, 6, 68
Somalia, 54-5, *80*, 90-1
South Africa, 25
Stanley, Sir Arthur, 13, *13*
Star & Garter Home, 13
Stark, Freya, *28*
steam launches, *24*, 42
Stone, Jonathan, 81
Sudan, 52-3

T

Taylor, Elizabeth, 87
Thailand, 52
Therapeutic Beauty Care, 71
Tobago, *20*
Tracing and Message Service, 68-9
training, 62
    air raid precautions, 623
    casualty faking, *64*
    manuals, 64-5
    modern, 63
trains, 25, *25*, *42*, 43
Transport and Escort service, 71

transportation, 423, 50-1
Treves, Sir Frederick, 12-13, *12*
Tristan da Cunha, *46*
Turco-Greek war, 75
Turkey, 24, 25

V

Victoria, Queen, 10, 82
Vietnam, 49
Voluntary Aid Detachments (VADs), 13,
    15, *15*, *26*, 27
    formation, 28-9, *28-9*
    fundraising, 77
    training, 62, *62*
Voluntary Medical Services Medal (VMS),
    16, 17

W

Wantage, Lord, 75
War Medal, *16*, 17
War Office, 15, 62
welfare work, 36-7
    overseas branches, 20
Weston, Simon, 87
Whitlam, Mike, *91*
Whittle, Mr, *11*
Wilson, Sheila, *57*
Winterbourne Gunner, 63
Wolseley, Sir Garnet, 24
workplace accidents, *63*
World War I, 8, 26-7
    fundraising, 75
    supplies, 50
    young members, 66
World War II, 32-7
    aftermath, 40
    fundraising, 76-7, 83
    Junior Red Cross, 67
Wounded and Missing Enquiry Bureau,
    69
Württemburg, 7

Y

Yarmouth, 30
Yemen war, 47
Yugoslavia, former *54*, 55, *59*, 81

Z

Zulu wars, 74

ACKNOWLEDGMENTS

The British Red Cross would like to thank John Gray, Director of Public Affairs, in particular (this project was his idea and he has given his support and advice throughout); Alison Kearns, Archivist, without whose knowledge and patience the work would never have been completed; all those who have taken the time to check through various parts of the book i.e. Lady Limerick (Sylvia), Chairman of Council, Mike Whitlam, Director General, and Margaret Poulter; in the Archives, Veronica Marchbanks, Helen Pugh, Antonia Moon, and Sian Wynn-Jones for giving so generously of their expert knowledge, on both text and photographs, on a constant basis; Mark O'Brien, Public Affairs, for his help with research and writing; Michael Meyer, Head of International Law, for his advice and help; Amanda Wheate, Publications, for helping throughout and particularly for taking on the task of organising approvals for the use of photographs; John Thompson, Publications, for helping with the copy; Naeem Khan, Library, for all his help with sourcing the modern photographs; Janice Sherwen, Arlene Heron and Sue McKinnon for helping to ensure the approval system worked as smoothly as possible; everyone else who has been pestered for information daily.

Dorling Kindersley would like to thank
Simon Albrow, for DTP work; Richard Bird, for the index; Alyson Kyles, for design assistance.

Special photography Tim Ridley

Photography and picture credits
British Red Cross/International Federation of Red Cross and Red Crescent Societies/International Committee of the Red Cross: p. 8 (btm left); p. 9 (btm right); p. 13 (top right); p. 14 (top left, btm left, mid right); p. 16 (btm left); p. 17 (top right); p. 20 (btm left, top mid); p. 21 (top right, mid left); p. 42 (top right, mid right); p. 43 (btm right); p. 45 (top right); p. 46 (top right); p. 47 (btm right); pp. 48-9 (top mid, btm left); p. 50 (top right, btm left); p. 51 (btm mid); p. 53 (btm mid, top left); p. 54 (top mid, btm left, mid left); p. 55 (btm left, top mid); p. 56 (btm left, btm right); p. 57 (top right, btm right, top mid); p. 59 (top left, top right, mid right, btm left); p. 60 (btm left); p. 63 (top right, btm right); p. 67 (top right, btm left); p. 70 (top right); p. 71 (top right, btm right); p. 72 (top left, btm right); p. 79 (top left); p. 80 (top right, btm left); p. 84 (top right); p. 86 (btm left); p. 87 (top right, btm left); p. 90 (btm left); p. 91 (top right); p. 92 (top left, btm right); p. 93 (btm right).
Picture agencies: p. 45 (btm right) The Sport and General Press Agency; p. 46 (btm left) Graham Studios, Covent Garden; p. 49 (btm right) Norwich Evening News; p. 51 (top right) Mike Perry, David Lipson Photographs, Dunmow; p. 52 (top right) Photo Color, Associated Press; p. 56 (top left) Yorkshire Television; p. 69 (btm right) Paul Lowe, Network; p. 81 (both) Rex Features; p. 84 (btm left) Simon Livingstone; p. 85 (top) Peterborough Evening Telegraph.
Thanks also to Selwyn Hutchinson for the pie chart on p. 88.

BRITISH RED CROSS

For further information or to offer help to the British Red Cross, get in touch with your local Branch Headquarters; you will find the number in the telephone directory or in the Yellow Pages.

National Headquarters
British Red Cross
9 Grosvenor Crescent
London SW1X 7EJ
0171-235 5454

Details of the royalties payable to the British Red Cross Society can be obtained by writing to the publisher Dorling Kindersley at the following address: 9 Henrietta Street, London WC2E 8PS

NOTE:

The illustrations on the cover commemorate the 125th birthday of the British Red Cross. The red cross emblem is a protective sign in armed conflicts

77798